The DRAGON'S TALE

By

TANIS HELLIWELL

Other books by Tanis Helliwell

The Leprechaun's Story: As told by Lloyd to Tanis Helliwell

Good Morning Henry: an in-depth journey with the body intelligence

High Beings of Hawaii: encounters with mystical ancestors

Hybrids: so you think you are human

Summer with the Leprechauns: a true story

Pilgrimage with the Leprechauns: a true story of a mystical
tour of Ireland

Decoding Your Destiny: keys to humanity's spiritual
transformation

Manifest Your Soul's Purpose

Embraced by Love: Poems

The DRAGON'S TALE

TANIS HELLIWELL

Published by Wayshower Enterprises

Library and Archives Canada Cataloguing in Publication

Title: The Dragon's Tale / by Tanis Helliwell.

Names: Helliwell, Tanis, author.

Identifiers: Canadiana (print) 20240344782 | Canadiana (ebook) 20240344820 | ISBN 9781987831481 (softcover) | ISBN 9781987831498 (Kindle) | ISBN 9781987831504 (EPUB)

Subjects: LCSH: Dragons. | LCSH: New Age movement. | LCSH: Spirituality.

Classification: LCC BP605.N48 H45 2024 | DDC 299/.93—dc23

Cover design by Nita Alvarez and Maywood Design.
Interior design and layout by Maywood Design.

Published by Wayshower Enterprises

https://www.tanishelliwell.com/
https://www.myspiritualtransformation.com/

To Mahavatar Babaji,
wayshower and prompter,
without whom this book
would never have been written.

Introduction

Dragons are real.

The Dragon's Tale is a true story of my encounters with dragons.

They are seldom seen as they exist in a higher frequency than our fast-paced, technological world. But that is changing as the possibility of other intelligent beings and their worlds are beginning to re-enter the consciousness of humanity.

If we are open to see, there is overwhelming evidence for the existence of dragons that has passed down through thousands of years of oral tradition. References to dragons go back more than 4,000 years in Sumeria, and ancient Mesopotamia, where the oldest written word for the dragon was written as 'usum-gal' (gal = big / usum = snake). The star, Alpha Draconis, which is the dragon's homeworld, is also called Thuban, the Arabic word for snake. Draconis is in the constellation of Draco, which was the Northern Pole star from 3942 until 1793 BCE, and many myths and stories about dragons stem from this time.

Around the world, and in many different languages, people have come up with words to describe dragons, but how they picture them, and whether they are regarded as friendly, or deadly, varies greatly across cultures. Dragons, in Chinese and Oriental mythology, are generally benevolent, wise, revered, and represent primal forces of Nature and the Universe. European dragons, on the other hand, are usually seen as malevolent. In Greek mythology, dragons were one of the species of Titans that the Olympian gods fought and replaced. In Christianity, dragons became identified with evil. Archangel Michael and St. George were often portrayed slaying dragons, which were associated with sexuality and early pagan beliefs.

In Mesoamerica, the dragon is found as the feathered serpent Quetzalcoatl. The worship of Quetzalcoatl began in the first century BCE and continued until Cortez arrived in America in the early sixteenth century. Quetzalcoatl is a Christ-like figure whose mother was said to be the Creator Mother God, Coatlicue, who formed all the stars of the Milky Way.

Quetzalcoatl was benevolent and credited with going to the underworld to create humanity for our current fifth-world cycle of evolution. He created humans from the bones of the previous races and by using his own blood. He brought civilization to humanity through the invention of books and the calendar, taught us to grow corn, and sometimes, was a symbol of death and resurrection.

Stories from all cultures say that dragons are beings of great power that know how to work with all four elements. A dragon can fly (air); swim (water); live in caves (earth); and breathe flames (fire).

Dragons, like angels and elementals, are real beings that exist in a higher frequency than us, which is why few of us have seen them. The Cosmic Dragon is a multi-dimensional being and the spiritual head of dragons, much as the Cosmic Christ is the spiritual head of humanity. The Cosmic Dragon, a being of great wisdom, is coming closer to us to watch and assist with the birth of the Earth and to welcome our planet into the community of conscious planets. The symbol of this process is found in the Chinese tradition and is depicted as a dragon encircling the cosmic egg.

Currently, the Cosmic Dragon is brooding the Earth, and the shell — the 'ring-pass-not' that surrounds Earth — is starting to crack. This Cosmic Dragon has the responsibility to open the ring-pass-not that protects inhabitants on other planets in our and other solar systems from humans … and us from them.

The Cosmic Dragon works with the kundalini energy of the Earth, the electromagnetic leylines, also known as dragon lines, to catalyze a rise in consciousness of the Earth. The Cosmic Dragon is bringing new cosmic energies into our solar system. It gathers the substances from the ethers, which are needed in the new age that we are entering. This divine being activates our higher chakras so we can enter an evolved state in our evolution. It works with the Karmic Board of humans to judge exactly when our pineal gland needs to be opened to awaken our dormant DNA. In this way, humanity will be prepared to access the cosmic information that has not been available until now.

When I began writing *The Dragon's Tale,* I had no idea that the coming year would welcome the Year of the Wood Dragon in Chinese astrology. The timing seemed significant. It was as if the Cosmic Dragons were, in some way, overseeing the book. In Chinese astrology, the dragon, when combined with the nourishing wood element, brings evolution, improvement, and abundance; it is the perfect time for rejuvenated beginnings and setting the foundation for long-term success. These are all qualities desperately needed in our beleaguered world and the message the dragons want humans to understand is they are here to help us.

Contents

Preface

A Long Ago Dream and Babaji's Message

I awaken in a cave. Still groggy from deep sleep, I purvey my surroundings wondering how I got there. There are two gigantic, thick pillars holding up the ceiling and when I look to my left, I notice an immense boulder. Confused, I attempt to understand where I am and slowly wander towards a large opening that I assume to be the way out. Peering down, I see I am many hundreds of feet in the air.

Immediately, I leap back and try to control my rising panic. How is this possible? Who brought me here? What has happened? Many questions and no answers. Withdrawing deeper into the cave, I look around for a door or other exit that could explain how I got here. Nothing. Turning around again to stare out the entrance, which appears to be my only hope of escape, I am stunned to see several dragons flying by at eye level. Red, blue, green, and bejeweled.

This is not a reassuring sight. Alone. Cave. Dragons. I turn around and look again at the large boulder I noticed when I awoke. It's egg-shaped. I examine the two pillars and discover that what I initially thought were outlines of bricks were scales and at the base of the pillars were clawed feet. Dragon feet.

At that moment, everything fell into place: I am in a dragon's cave being brooded by a dragon! And soon, a baby dragon — much larger than me, given the size of the egg — will emerge from that boulder. My heart stops in fear. Breathless, I wake up.

I can remember every detail of that very real conscious vision, even though it happened 30 years ago. Sometimes, conscious dreams and visions stay in the past and sometimes they affect the present. That is what happened to me.

One year ago, something completely unexpected and life-changing occurred. I was meditating and greeting each of the masters associated with my meditation practice. One of the masters is Mahavatar Babaji, the deathless guru who lives in the Himalayas and who has appeared to many advanced students over hundreds of years. Usually, when I see him, he is about my height, which is very short for a man, and he taps me on the top of my head, but he has never spoken to me.

On this occasion, however, he grew within milliseconds to an incredible height and pulled me up with him until we were in an astral universe where I could see the Earth and two other inhabited planets. He said to me, "You have done enough for the elementals." Then, looking right towards one of the other planets, Mahavatar Babaji continued, "Have you thought about dragons?"

Profoundly shocked, I immediately opened my eyes to find myself back in my physical body... gasping for air. I realized what a tremendous honor that Babaji was speaking to me and giving me an assignment. Yet I had devoted 30 years to writing books about elementals and their world and didn't relish the responsibility of writing about a new and entirely different realm of existence.

Still, I couldn't deny that many significant interventions by dragons had occurred during my life. Nor could I ignore a request from Babaji who had asked Paramahansa Yogananda to write his many books. Babaji had never requested anything from me previously and I trusted that he would only ask for something that would be good for others as well as myself. Nevertheless, I stalled in making a decision.

One week later, while meditating, Babaji, once again, pulled me energetically into the astral universe where he repeated his previous request. This time I didn't feel as overwhelmed and took the opportunity to look around. Hovering in this high plane, I saw three worlds: the Earth, the Dragon planet, and another planet, which I intuitively knew was the world for Merpeople — where mermaids and mermen dwell. I glimpsed a larger universe spreading beyond those three worlds, but knew it was not my task to write about that.

Returning my attention to the dragon world, I felt pulled by a being who wished to communicate with me. An instant later, I was in the presence of a large, magnificent dragon and knew it was waiting patiently for us to begin the book that Babaji had requested. The dragon felt familiar although I was unsure if it was the mother dragon or its offspring in the egg that I had glimpsed many decades ago. The question remained unanswered as I opened my eyes.

Dragons
and
The Earth

Meeting the Dragon

A year had passed since Mahavatar Babaji's request and, although I occasionally thought about attempting to speak with the dragons, I was occupied with other projects and didn't feel a sense of urgency. Neither a request from Babaji nor a never-forgotten visionary dream was enough to stir me into action. This was about to change.

I was in France getting ready to teach at the ashram of a Dutch guru friend of mine. I first met Prajnaparamita about eight years ago in the Netherlands. She was there leading *satsangs*, which are gatherings of people seeking spiritual truth, either in dialogue or proximity, with an enlightened master. I had never attended one of Prajnaparamita's satsangs and was surprised when she told one of her devotees that she would like to meet me.

The day arrived and I prepared to meet her by bringing a *kata*, a white scarf symbolizing purity and compassion. In the Tibetan Buddhist tradition, the guru blesses the kata and then returns it to you so that you receive the blessing. I was waiting with my friend as Prajnaparamita's car pulled up. When she emerged from the driver's side, my first thought was what a modern guru she must be to drive herself. She was dressed totally in white and her wavy blond hair framed a widely smiling face. Like a lion on good behavior, she exuded power and will at the same time as her blue eyes flashed with intelligence and curiosity. Prajnaparamita was a full-bodied woman with a great deal of physical energy and I was warmed by the smile with which she greeted me.

Slowly walking forward, I held out the kata in open hands expecting her to bless it and then place it around my neck. Taking the gift, and, still smiling, she placed it around her own neck. She then held out another prayer scarf, one that contained a lovely crystal with which she blessed me. Her actions were unusual and unexpected as they symbolized that we were meeting as friends and comrades living a spiritual life and not as devotee and guru. Over the next years, Prajnaparamita and I met in the Netherlands whenever both of us were there and she invited me to her ashram to teach about elementals, hybrids, and body-spirit consciousness.

You may be wondering why an enlightened guru would invite a person like me to teach about beings in the astral world. Isn't it a guru's purpose to assist others to wake up to the Truth that all form is imagined and illusionary? And doesn't my teaching about the astral realms reinforce a belief in them and, therefore, tempt others to seek experiences in these realms? That's the question I initially asked myself. However, upon looking deeper, I realized there was no conflict between Prajnaparamita's work and mine. All realms, including physical, astral, and causal worlds of form, are various aspects of Spirit, thus journeying through them to consciousness is a viable way to know Spirit. My gift is assisting others to become conscious in these various worlds of form and Prajnaparamita's gift is to show others who they truly are and accompany them as a guide on the spiritual path. Furthermore,

Prajnaparamita's expertise not only helps free her devotees from the physical world, but encourages them to fully embrace it by filling her ashram with beautiful trees and lush, healthy gardens.

That's the background for how eight years later, I arrived at her ashram, La Roseraie de Sacha, in France to teach several short workshops. The ashram is 24 hectares, which is about 60 acres, and the morning after I arrived, Prajnaparamita took me on a tour of the food gardens, orchards, and power places on the property.

I thought we were winding down the tour when she looked at me and said, "A few years ago two pandits from my spiritual lineage in India came to La Roseraie de Sacha. They blessed our ashram with many ceremonies and *havans*. Accompanying the pandits was a devotee of my Guru who sees subtle realms and, during one of the ceremonies, he observed a black dragon arriving in our forest gracing La Roseraie de Sacha. We leave that area alone; however, I'd like to take you to see what you discover."

Hearing her words, I was certain the dragon had come for me. As we walked along the overgrown path through the forest, I had time to reflect on how both my long-ago dream and instructions by Babaji had brought me to the present moment. I could no longer postpone this meeting. We arrived at a thickly wooded, uncleared, and abandoned part of the forest.

Turning towards me, Prajnaparamita said, "We are told this is where the dragon is resting. I've asked the others not to come to this place, but I'd like to hear about anything you learn."

I felt the dragon waiting for me in the shadows and knew that it wanted to speak with me alone. I turned to Prajnaparamita and said, "It's not by accident the dragon and I are both here. In two unforgettable experiences, I was taken by Mahavatar Babaji into a high astral frequency where he pointed at a strange planet and said, 'You've written enough about elementals. What about dragons?' For exactly a year this month, I've known I would need to honor his request, but I wanted to complete my other projects. I guess my grace time is over and I now must act."

We backed away from the place the dragon was lairing and, turning around, left the forest. I needed to prepare to speak with the dragon, I intuitively knew our conversations would continue during my time there. I no longer felt reluctant to begin and a gentle excitement to learn something new was arising in me. And the timing was perfect as I was teaching in the afternoons and had mornings free to be with the dragon.

The first afternoon arrived and the participants were gathered in a circle in the orchard. I joined them and sat in an empty chair, obviously meant for me, as Prajnaparamita sat in the chair to my left. I was to teach about elementals as this was of special interest to many of the participants who had a special interest in them. I began and was going through the various kinds of elementals that might wish to become their elemental partners when suddenly John, one of the participants, asked, "This is a place of dragons. What does that mean for us?"

John had been a part of the ashram for over ten years and knew what the devotee had said about the dragon and where it had landed. However, Prajnaparamita had told me earlier that she didn't wish me to discuss the topic of dragons on the property, so I wasn't sure how to respond.

Glancing towards Prajnaparamita, I quickly understood her 'don't discuss it now' look.

Turning back to John, I said, "It's not the time to discuss this as dragons are not elementals. Let's get back to elementals."

I returned to the day's topic and led the participants in a visualization to receive elemental partners, so all continued pleasantly. Despite that, I felt uncomfortable that I hadn't given John a straight answer. Then, a solution came to me and, when the session ended, I spoke with Prajnaparamita.

"I'm going to need help carrying a chair and other things into the forest to speak with the dragon," I said. "I was wondering if I could ask John to help?"

"Yes, that would be fine," she answered. "I just don't want the topic of the dragon to be discussed in the group right now."

John is a reticent, quiet man of middle height, weight, and age. He conveys a sense that he is always eager to help wherever help is needed, and is also happy to slide into the background. Later, I approached John, "Could you meet me tomorrow at 9 a.m.?"

He looked puzzled so I continued, "I need you to help me carry a chair and some pillows into the part of the forest where the dragon is residing."

A man of few words, John nodded and I knew he would be there with what I wanted the following morning.

I awoke early to the sound of little birds singing their hearts out. A beautiful breeze wafted through the bedroom window. Lying in bed, I contemplated the day with mixed feelings. On one level, I was excited to learn more about dragons and what they wanted to share. On the other hand, I worried that I may not be competent because I had never spoken with dragons before. Old feelings of failure arose, to be greeted by an equally strong eagerness and a deep trust in my vision with Babaji. After all, if he knew I could do it, how could I doubt myself? I was strengthened by my confidence in him and how circumstances had followed me for over 30 years to bring me to this place of meeting the dragon again. But which dragon would I meet? Would it be the mother who brooded me or the one in the egg that was my nestmate?

Breakfast was a hurried affair and I busied myself getting my cell phone ready to record any conversation with the dragon and a notebook to begin writing. Right at 9 a.m., a knock at the door announced John's arrival and we set off in silence. Thank heavens he didn't want to talk, I thought to myself, so that I could remain calm and centered for the upcoming meeting. Even though I have been a mystic my entire life and have seen many astral realms, I had a deep knowing that I would have to access much higher frequencies to understand everything the dragon would say. In other words, it would be a spiritual stretch.

Preoccupied with my thoughts, I was surprised at how quickly we left the sunny meadows to enter the dark forest where silence reigned. John suddenly stopped and waited to see how I wanted to proceed. I signaled him to walk ahead, so I could remain in a quiet, meditative state. Following the same path that Prajnaparamita had taken the previous day, we soon arrived at the dragon's lair.

"Where shall I put the chair?" John asked softly, as this was a place of hushed voices.

"Right here and turn it towards those trees," I replied, waving him towards the place where I knew the dragon rested.

John carefully placed the chair in a level place and faced it in the direction where the dragon lay. He could see nothing, but I'm sure he felt its presence. Having done as requested, he carefully backed down the path until I could no longer hear him. I was alone. I tentatively sat down and, putting my notebook on the ground, closed my physical eyes to open my third eye, the eye I use to see in higher realms.

Immediately, I saw a large indigo dragon with golden eyes and fierce intelligence staring back at me. A wild creature, untamed, gigantic, and not something to which I could easily relate. And yet, somehow, I felt I would be safe.

The dragon was coiled with its massive tail around its body in a relaxed position. Its elegant head, broad at the forehead with a slim nose, was as large as my entire body and its nostrils were open and widespread. Its mouth was similar to that of a flesh-eating dinosaur, complete with sharp teeth. It had a rough flap of feathery-looking skin hanging a little back from its chin and continuing down its throat. And above its large eyes were tuffs that resembled eyebrows. Its ears were elfen-like in that they were long and pointed with a flap that could close when the dragon was submerged in water, sleeping, or blocking unpleasant sounds. Its long, flexible neck was heavily muscled to hold up its large head. Its body was well formed, neither fat nor skinny, and it appeared to weigh many tons.

The dragon patiently allowed my examination and, when I telepathically asked it to stand so I could determine the length of its body, it complied with good grace. Its body without the tail was easily 15 or more feet long and its four strong, scaled legs were like solid tree trunks. Its feet were not delicate but muscular and capable of holding heavy weights, while each of its five talons was as long as my forearm. The dragon's body was blue-black, blacker on top, with iridescent indigo blue on its belly. This color continued down its legs but did not extend to the flesh-colored talons.

On either side of the dragon's body were two gigantic wings. They resembled a folding fan with a hinged double joint, so they could compress easily against the dragon's body when it lay or stood at rest. I could see the importance of that feature to maneuver within the dense trees where the dragon chose to rest. As I studied its wings, the dragon sent me a telepathic image of their full extension. Each one was double the size of its body. When open, they were a rich indigo color flecked with red and other rich jewel tones, which shone like gems. Its long, scaled tail was the same length as its body. The tail was forked at the end and shaped like a flat rudder with a vertical piece that allowed the dragon to steer itself through the air.

Having studied its body in great detail, I returned my attention to its intense golden eyes — like those of a snake with a black center. As I did this, the dragon, knowing my examination was complete, relaxed into a resting position calculated to make itself as unintimidating as possible. It waited for me to enter a calm, inner state before addressing me.

"I've been waiting for you to come to my world to speak with me," the dragon began pointedly. "You have delayed; hence I've come to speak with you. There is a hole through space and time that allows me to come here from Draconis where I live."

Its voice was low and deep and it spoke quietly, so as not to overwhelm me. I did not feel it was scolding me… merely conveying a fact. This allowed me to remain receptive and calm as I waited for the dragon to continue.

"We've never met. I was the being in the egg that our mother brooded. We are nest siblings. You are my nest sister even though you are such a different being from me. Our mother took the memories of all the dragons and our sire catalyzed these memories to create me. In this way, information about dragons and our world would awaken in me at my birth. This, we dragons can do. We can decide what memories from our ancestors we will keep and pass on to our offspring. We can remember our ancestors even back to the beginning ancestor. And we can recite the lineage. When a new being is to be born, we strengthen the memories that are most important for the being to know to fulfill its purpose. Our mother was chosen for this reason. Because she is a wisdom keeper of the indigo lineage, she could hold these memories stronger and longer than other dragons. Some dragon lineages are newer, but ours is ancient."

As the dragon spoke, it became obvious that 'it' was a 'he' and that he was going to become my main contact. I was disappointed for a few reasons. I would have preferred to speak with what he referred to as our brood mother who, according to him, was wise. He was a youngster, so how much could he know anyway? And to be honest, I was overwhelmed with the size of any dragon and thought a female might have been a bit smaller.

"You're disappointed that you didn't get our mother," he said. "That wasn't possible because I'm the spokesperson for the dragons to the humans. This is the role that I've been preparing for throughout many lifetimes. You will be able to speak with our mother and members of other lineages once you and I know each other more."

He so fully knew my thoughts that I realized I wouldn't be able to keep anything from him. Unfortunately, I couldn't hear everything he was thinking.

"But you can hear what I'm thinking," he said, commenting, once again, on my unspoken thoughts. "Let me explain. Thoughts are in layers. It's easy to hear current and strong thoughts as they lie near the surface of your mind. This is why I could hear what you've been thinking in my presence. It's more difficult to hear older, or deeply embedded, even forgotten thoughts. I can do this too, but it takes more effort. Our old dragons can hear all your remembered and not-remembered thoughts with no effort at all."

"I can hear what you're saying even though you aren't using words," I said. "I see images and hear thoughts. Is this how you dragons do it?"

"You hear what I want you to hear because I project my thoughts towards you," he replied. "You wouldn't be able to hear what I don't project. I, like all dragons, can hear what is hidden or dormant inside you. However, I must say it's a tangled mess of thoughts and feelings inside humans, whereas it's clear and precise inside dragons."

"And could that be because we are different races?" I asked, trying not to be offended.

"Partially," he granted. "Dragons dwell in higher frequencies and have learned in our long history to still our emotions and thoughts. Humans will learn to do this, too."

I was considering what he was saying when he announced, "That's enough for today. Your focus is not as good as it could be and we need to go slowly for you to move into the higher frequency where dragons live. Come here tomorrow morning."

With those last words, I was dismissed. I left my chair, which John would pick up later, and retreated. As I wound my way back through the forest and meadows to the comfort of my room, I digested what the dragon had said. He was a male and, according to him, my nest brother, but what exactly did he mean by that term? How interesting that he referred to his mother as 'our' mother. I'm a human, not a dragon, so I wondered at his choice of words. Yet, it was true that I'd seen myself in their cave in my meditations.

I was curious to hear more from him and eager to discover my purpose in that world. If he was the one chosen to communicate with me, the human, was I the one chosen to communicate with him, the dragon, and, if so, what was next?

The answers to these questions would have to wait. Although the dragon had maintained a monologue in our first meeting, I intuitively felt that we would continue with a dialogue soon, as our first meeting was more of an introduction. I guess that's the way dragons do it. I had a lot to learn.

The Dragon
and Sacred Fire

That night we had a fire ceremony in the little octagonal building made of strawbales and mud on the edge of the forest not far from where the dragon was. A *havan*, as it's known in India, is a blessing for all those who attend and the prayers and mantras spiral out and bless the world and the spirit worlds. This *havan* was a powerful event led by three devotees, one of whom was John. All three had been trained by pandits from Prajnaparamita's lineage and had been offering ceremonies for 20 years. The three devotees offered incense, ghee, grain, and other things to the fire and led us in chanting and honoring great beings and the elementals on the land and I prayed for a blessing for the dragon.

During the ceremony, each of the three devotees chose one-third of our group to bless by placing the sacred ashes from the fire on our third eye. John came to bless me. As he was placing the ashes on my forehead, I heard the dragon's voice interrupting my meditation, "Bring the ashes to me tomorrow morning."

His voice hovered somewhere between a request and a demand. I was not offended because I realized he was treating me the way he would communicate with one of his own.

As Prajnaparamita and I were exiting the building after the ceremony, I turned to John and said, "Please leave the chair in the *havan* with the ashes and, together, we will carry them to the forest tomorrow."

Never a man of many words, John nodded his assent.

The next morning at 9 a.m. sharp, there was a light knock at my door.

Together we carried the ashes and chair into the forest and, arriving at the dragon's lair, John asked, "Where do you wish me to place the ashes?"

I turned to request what he wanted and the dragon rose to his feet. Bending his head over his breast, he indicated that the ashes be placed on the ground directly in front of him. I asked John to do this.

Moving cautiously forward and bowing in reverence, he positioned the ashes exactly where requested. Having done this, still bowing, he backed out until he stood again with me.

I thanked John and waited for him to leave the forest. I wasn't attempting to be secretive, but I knew that both the dragon and Prajnaparamita wanted only me there.

When the dragon was satisfied that we were alone, he started consuming the ashes with great relish, accompanied by many sighs of pleasure. Finished, he lay down so that he didn't dwarf me with his size and, looking at me, began his discourse.

"Ingesting these ashes blessed by a healing fire catalyzes the memories of the ancestors of my lineage as well as those of all dragon lineages. This will assist me to recount their history, their lineage, and how they are working with the Earth. Last night, you put your prayers into the fire and burnt them with oil. You sang to invite human masters to come and consecrate the fire. You asked for a

. the elementals, the land, and one for me. I'm grateful
ʌomage."

ɪow do you know everything that happened?" I asked in awe.

'Everything that transpired is in the ashes I consumed and in your
thoughts," he replied. "We're not elementals who wish to play and
have fun with you, nor are we spontaneous like them. We're wisdom
holders. Deep thinkers. We travel in the depths of space between
worlds and some of us even travel between galaxies along the grid of
light that we call dragon lines. We do this through deep concentration."

Many questions were lurking in my mind as he spoke. The
dragon, sensing this, stopped and gave me a 'Don't say anything
look?' which was, as you can imagine, enough to put me into
listening mode again.

"Dragons have come to your planet for eons," he continued, "from
the time it first burst from idea into form. We're here to catalyze the
birth of the Earth…to lend our wisdom and fire energy to the process.
With our sacred fire, which we breathe forth from our being, we
sparked consciousness into form and lit this in the etheric memory
of the Earth. This, we knew, would grow and evolve in time to create
all the life forms that you have had, that you currently have, and that
you will have in the future. This is our mission — not only with your
planet, but with many evolving races in this universe.

"We've been given this mission by the one you call God, the
Creator. We call the Creator the Source of All. The Source of All is
the source of our fire and, unlike the external fire you created in the
ceremony last evening, we create a sacred fire within ourselves. Even
a small, newly birthed dragon hatchling can create a spark. It's born
with all the raw material within itself to do this. We emerged from the

Source of All embodying the ability to hold the four elements of earth, air, fire, water, and even more elements, both in balance and in form.

"When I say form," he continued, "I don't mean only the physical, three-dimensional reality in which you are conscious of form. We work in 12 dimensions and some of the great, great ones — the masters among us, the timeless ones — travel from galaxy to galaxy. There are 12 dimensions in this galaxy and there are even higher dimensions beyond this."

Although I was intrigued by what he was saying, I was overwhelmed by the speed with which he spoke and kept feeling that I was falling behind.

He immediately picked up my problem and said, "I hear you reflecting on my words and I sense limitations in fully understanding what my words mean. I will breathe my essence into you and bless you that you may travel with me in understanding."

The dragon didn't wait for my assent and gave me no time to be afraid of what breathing his essence into me might entail. Instead, he took a big breath and exhaled over me. His breath rustled through my hair and across my face and created a breeze through the nearby trees. Thank God, there was no actual fire, I thought. Instead, it felt as if he had breathed a blessing similar to what I have previously felt from the Holy Spirit.

"Your breath feels like that of the Holy Spirit, the same Holy Spirit that appeared on the heads of the disciples of Jesus on Pentecost," I said to the dragon, breaking my enforced silence. "I find this interesting as we are only a few days from Pentecost and I've had many experiences being blessed with fire on that day."

The dragon waited patiently for me to finish speaking and I was relieved that he didn't seem offended that I'd spoken. Legendary stories say that dragons are proud, so perhaps he didn't mind as I was complimenting his fire blessing. He looked at me smiling an amused smile and answered.

"In early, early times we breathed on humans and other beings to catalyze their awakenings, their evolution, their development, their wisdom. Then as the evolution of humanity progressed, humans became afraid of our fire and no longer wanted our blessing. They wanted to go their own way. Humans began to feel we were a danger, a threat, and that we were evil. For this reason, you created stories of wanting to kill dragons. So, for millennia upon millennia, we haven't been brothers and sisters on the path to return to the Source of All.

"When I say to return to the Source of All, I don't mean it in the small way that you understand which is: that to become enlightened, you must sacrifice your identity and collapse into divinity. No, no, no! It's not the same for us.

"You wish this because humans have gone so badly astray in your evolution that you have a deep longing to return to what you call Eden, to the innocence of being in the Source of All. Humans have a deep self-loathing, although none of you are aware of this."

"Why do we have self-loathing?" I inquired before he could say more. I was determined that our communication would be a dialogue, not a monologue.

He smiled indulgently, if baring his teeth could be a smile. His smile was the lenient tolerance of a wise, older being who knew what I thought and felt long before I did.

"Why do we have self-loathing?" I repeated, stubbornly clinging to my wish to have a dialogue. "Can you tell me why?"

His smile stretched into forbearing patience.

"You humans feel guilty for what you've wrought on this beautiful planet," he replied to my question. "This is why you have the desire to surrender all you have become to return to the heart of the Source where you wish to remain. Hmmm ... Hmmm ... And some of you, you call them *bodhisattvas*, wish to reincarnate again into conscious awareness to help all those humans still struggling on the path and to repay the debt you feel you owe."

I was reflecting on what he said and wanted to acknowledge the truth in his words when he steered me in another direction.

"I know you understand what I'm saying, Tanis. Your name Tanis is interesting. Do you hear the 's' of the snake? The 's' in Tanis indicates that you hold snake energy."

"What 's' of what snake?" I asked, unsure if this was desirable in human terms.

"Snakes and dragons are related. We are their ancestors. You might recall that dragons have been called snakes in your myths," he replied, in a 'see how smart I am' grin calculated to impress me with his knowledge of humans.

"Before we go any further, I have a question that won't wait," I interrupted. "You seem to know my name, but I don't know yours. I can't keep on calling you 'the dragon'. What is your name?"

"You couldn't pronounce it," he responded, shrugging his huge shoulders and exhaling with a 'woe is me that I have to communicate with this human' attitude.

"Try," I insisted.

"Here goes. It's Jaakelousekindvron," he replied, leaving me to figure out the spelling, given that there were many huffs and grunts in between the letters.

"Thanks," I said happily. "I have an idea to make it easier for this dullard human to call you by name. Humans — as you being a smart dragon must know — often have nicknames. How about I call you Jake?"

Squinting his eyes, he glared at me so intently that I wondered if I'd committed a terrible blunder and badly insulted him.

Noticing the effect he was having, he broke into laughter, "Hahaha...that is perfect. I like it. Yes, I accept Jake as my human nickname...but what does it mean? Dragon names always capture the essence of the dragon and I want to make sure the name Jake suits me."

"In our Old English myths, the name 'drake' was used for a young male dragon that had just left the nest."

"Continue..." he said, patiently postponing judgment.

"Drake suits what you are as a dragon; yet, it's too impersonal if we are going to develop our relationship. After all, if you are my dragon brother, which, by the way, I don't quite understand yet, I'd like to call you by name."

I left my question hanging and hoped he would tell me more about our relationship, but he didn't pick up my desire, and said instead, "Tell me more about my name?"

"Humans, like dragons, need the right name and Jake sprang to mind. It means humanitarian and you are working with a human. Furthermore, it means generous, honest, brilliant, inventive, inspired. Do you think this name describes you?" I replied.

"Absolutely," he said with a smile.

I realized he was basking in the joy of trying out something typically human, but I had another pressing question.

"A minute ago, Jake," I said, trying out his nickname, "you were talking about our human desire to return to Eden. In our biblical stories, myths you might call them, we state that the snake tempted us to leave Eden by telling us to eat from the Tree of Knowledge. Was the snake a dragon?"

"Definitely," Jake said. "However, we don't view ourselves in the negative way in which your myths have cast us. We were working in Eden, which is a higher vibratory realm, to catalyze your kundalini energy to move you into wisdom. This was done in keeping with our dragon gift on behalf of the Source of All, which you refer to as God.

"You hold this energy," he repeated, steering our conversation back to what he wanted to say. "The kundalini energy, this dragon energy, is through your mother's lineage. Yes, yes, yes! Through your father's lineage too. This is why we've chosen you to ground this message in your world. You will do this through writing a book. We know that you did this for over 20 years by taking individuals to sacred sites located on the dragon lines of the Earth. You blessed these sites and opened their energy to heal the Earth. These dragon lines are the equivalent of the kundalini energy in your body."

"I've always felt they were related," I commented. "That's why when we meditated or did rituals at sacred sites along these dragon lines, we also were healed. Are these power nodes, such as Newgrange in Ireland and the Pyramid of Giza in Egypt, the equivalent of chakras in the human body?"

"Correct. And working with these energies have catalyzed your spiritual energy," Jake acknowledged. "However, there are limitations in your understanding and I will help you to better understand dragon consciousness.

"Dragons are masters of the four elements of earth, air, fire, and water, but there are elements in higher frequencies that humans have discover. We work with these elements as well. The collective consciousness of dragons, of which I am but a spokesperson, a messenger, seeks to transmute these higher elements. In your terms, we are alchemists transmuting your equivalent of lead into gold, or coal into a diamond."

"I'm trying to follow you," I confessed. "Could you give an example to which I can relate?"

"Alright!" he responded. "There are crystals in your pineal gland and these crystals grow mostly in wisdom as you humans evolve in consciousness. Dragons differ in that crystal is throughout our dragon minds. We don't use the word brain as you do because we're not solid in the way you conceive of solid."

"Okay, I'm with you so far. Can you speak more about these crystals in your mind?"

"Of course," Jake replied.

His eyes were animated as he spoke and I noticed how happy he was to share his advanced wisdom. "Each cell within our dragon body has these crystals. When I say crystals, don't think of physical rock crystals. We mean the essence of which the crystals are made in higher frequencies. These crystals are throughout our entire body. They are in the human body too, but they lie dormant at this time. These crystals are beginning to awaken in humanity and this process will continue during the next 2000 years of what you term the 'Aquarian Age'. Dragons are helping to catalyze these dormant crystals in humanity to help you to evolve to higher frequencies."

"Is there anything in my experience that would help me relate to what you mean by humans having these crystals in our body in higher frequencies?" I asked hopefully.

"Indeed," he answered, sending me a penetrating look. "In waking dreams and deep meditation, when you see highly evolved spiritual friends and masters in the astral world, you notice that their eyes often look like whirling crystal lights. They are what all humans will become, this crystal life."

"You're correct. I do often see these beings in the astral world with crystal eyes, but how did you know that?"

"If I focus, I can see exactly what you see — not only physically, but in higher frequencies," he replied. "However, don't distract me. I want to explain about dragons. Dragons store memory in our entire body using live crystals, although there is a more concentrated focus in our head area. Why? Because we, like humans, developed more in the head area in our evolution. But the longer we have been evolving and the older we are, the more these crystals are distributed throughout our entire bodies.

"And as we age," he continued, "we grow larger. Some of the great, great, great old ones are, in your terms, immense — larger than an ocean liner."

Jake started to chortle at some inner joke so, hoping to share his amusement, I asked, "What's so funny?"

"It amuses me to compare our great ones with an ocean liner and my association is valid because they travel between the stars. So in that way, old dragons are like a conscious ocean liner."

He must have heard me wondering if I'd be fortunate enough to meet any of these old ones because he interrupted my reverie.

"You have asked why such a young one like me would be the one to talk to you. Hmmm...Hmmm... mainly because of two things. Well, I could say ten things, but not to overwhelm you, I'll give you two. First of all, our mother is of the wisdom keeper lineage. She was given the memories of all dragon lineages, so I would be born with all their memories. Dragons prefer to only hold the memories of their lineage and it's a burden for me to hold memories of all lineages.

"Secondly, our sire is a very old dragon and he catalyzed these memories. The old ones, who travel between stars, hold the memories of all lineages. However, I was given just a little bit. In your terms, you would call it a homeopathic dose. I was prepared. They built this form. They created it purposefully. The Source of All oversees this process so I could come with these homeopathic doses into the Earth frequencies to speak with you. And when I say Earth frequency, I don't mean the physical Earth. I address you from the high astral and lower causal frequencies. This realm is very subtle where we create form with thought. Before this time, you would not have been ready to receive these energies, these memories. You were too dense, too cluttered, and your mind was not clear enough. Now you are ready. That is enough for today. Tomorrow, we continue."

Dismissed, I wandered blurrily back through the forest and home to lie down. It took a great deal of energy to continue these interviews or whatever they were. Actually, they felt more like transmissions or teachings. Although he allowed me to ask questions, I knew that my mind worked very slowly for him and that, telepathically, he knew my thoughts and feelings before I did.

How Dragons Travel in Space and Time

The next morning, I rose early and did my energization exercises before going to the temple for 7 a.m. meditation. The residents in the ashram recite the Gayatri mantra to start each day. Although Prajnaparamita told me that it was not necessary to go and that she didn't participate, I felt drawn to join them because of the power of their meditation.

The Gayatri mantra first uttered in the Rig Veda is dedicated to the Source of All, the Creator, also called the Great Central Sun, in gratitude for our life. Although reciting the Gayatri Mantra has not been part of my meditation practice, I sat in silence among them and allowed waves of blessing to wash over me. Gratitude filled my heart — not only for my life but also that I had come to the ashram. After the recitation ended, we sat in silence for another 30 minutes which allowed me time to meditate and gather my thoughts for the coming day.

I now knew that my mornings would be dedicated to speaking with Jake and I was fortunate that I didn't need to teach until the afternoons. Prajnaparamita led satsangs in the evening, so I was able to enjoy a wonderful balance of meditation, learning about dragons, teaching what I had come to share, and ingesting spiritual food in the evenings.

John was waiting for me at 9 a.m. and together we walked to the havan building to get my chair. By now it was clear to both of us that the smart thing was to leave the chair there, rather than carry it daily from my little abode. I realized John was curious to know what the dragon was saying; however, he respectfully didn't interrupt my silence. When we arrived at the havan building, he gathered up the chair, carried it into the forest, and placed it in its usual place facing the direction in which he knew the dragon crouched. Silently, he backed away leaving me alone.

This morning, before addressing Jake, I decided to call on the lineage of Masters with whom I meditate. I thought if they assisted me, it would be easier to receive the transmission.

Immediately, Jake became upset and, shaking his head in annoyance, said, "This is not the place to call on human masters as their energy is different from mine and what I wish to convey. It creates a block rather than a path between us."

Shocked at his reaction, I answered, "How can that be when it's Mahavatar Babaji who pointed me toward your world to ask if I would consider speaking with you dragons?"

"That may be," he replied, "however, he didn't bring you to our world, did he? He just pointed you there."

"I don't doubt that he could go to your world in a second," I retorted. "He would have a more intimate connection with you in your so-called advanced evolution than I could ever hope to have."

"In that you are correct," he granted. "The energy of great masters, such as Babaji, is no longer human. It's not any particular lineage anymore. They have returned to the Source of All and can travel in space and time as we do. However, and this is a big however, every human master has his or her note and specific vibration. Their notes, when you think of the masters in their human form, are not fully aligned to our dragon resonance."

"That's interesting," I said, eager to understand. "Could you explain why their vibrations are not aligned?"

"It's like having a grove of apple trees and you plant a cherry tree in the middle. The cherry tree doesn't belong in the grove of apple trees. The evolutionary path, which human masters have taken, is imprinted on them as it is with all races, even when they return to the Source of All."

"I've always thought that would be the case," I acknowledged, "so I'm reassured by what you say. If that is the case, how do you keep your note when speaking to me, a human? Isn't my note, my vibration, difficult for you?"

"For me to keep my note pure and hold my dragon's resonance together for you, it's better that you don't call on human masters because the way you identify with them is through their human personalities. When you think of them and their human teachings, it's not in resonance with our dragon lineage. Is that clear?"

I was unsettled by his request as, in the back of my mind, I wanted to reassure myself that human masters would protect me from anything the dragon — my 'so called' nest brother included — said that wasn't aligned with my human lineage.

Knowing my thoughts, Jake wanted to put me at ease. "If you cannot pray to the human masters to protect you from me, it increases your suspicion of me, doesn't it."

"Of course, it does," I replied and added, "Why is that and do you have a solution that I can trust?"

"You're suspicious not only because I'm a dragon but also because I'm an indigo-black color that you associate with the ray of magic. This comes from your knowledge of black magicians who stole power from others. You're right in your human reference, I am on the ray of magic. But to say that I'm evil is not helpful. I'm already different enough from your evolution that to create any blocks between us — other than what we already have in differences — will prevent a clear transmission."

"You're correct that I'm suspicious of those on the ray of magic because of black magicians. What can you say to help relieve me of this suspicion?"

"Simply, you're prejudiced. You have a block. Get over it!"

As Jake spoke, he sent me a strong telepathic image of how he perceived my clinging to old prejudices and I could see through his eyes that I was being stubborn and even childish. Seeing this image of myself was amazingly helpful and I was able to extend this vision to other ways in which I might be holding on to old prejudices that needed to be reconsidered.

He waited patiently before he spoke again. "Indigo dragons who carry the magic note, or vibration, if you prefer that word, are the ones who travel through deep space. The void of deep space is where unmanifested potential exists. We travel to other galaxies by thinking of where we want to go. We are the law keepers of other evolving races. We create star paths between worlds and other civilizations. Other planets. Other solar systems. Galaxies. We've learned a degree of flexibility because we come into contact with so many races. This flexibility is what allows me to speak with you, to make myself understood in your limited human terms. Dragons have used telepathy for a long time. So for us, although you have excellent development as a human, you are still a fledgling. This is why a fledgling was chosen to speak with you. You could not talk to an old one at this moment."

I wasn't greatly impressed both by being considered limited and his arrogant tone. He immediately picked up on my displeasure and attempted to humor me.

"Perhaps, as we deepen our connection and share our essence, the time will come when you can speak with an old one. Certainly, it's predicted that you will speak with our mother. When I say predicted, you think it's pre-ordained."

"That's correct, I do think this. Do you understand these terms differently?" I inquired, confused.

"We see the destiny of what will happen whereas humans, with their concept of free will, attempt to control every step of the choices they make. Humans ask, 'What do I choose?' 'Which direction do I go in?' 'Do I step back?' 'Do I step forward?' Humans engage in so much lost energy. For dragons, it's different. We feel our preordained destiny in every crystal in our body. To realize my destiny, I only needed to see myself here speaking with you for it to happen. This is the way humans will ultimately travel and, by going to the past and the future, you have already experienced this. Nonetheless, you and humanity are still taking early steps. For us dragons, it's the normal means of travel, whereas for you humans, it's an exceptional moment when this happens."

"I'm wondering if the ability to travel into the past and future by using guided visualizations is a step in the right direction towards your ability to travel in space and time?"

"There are graduations," Jake answered. "Visualization is the first step and physically transporting yourself into another time where you've had an incarnation is a further step.

"Advanced human masters, such as Mahavatar Babaji and Jesus, were able to physically appear in more than one place and be seen by many people at the same time. Is this an even more developed step?" I asked.

"This is more what I'm speaking of," he replied. "And your work with the body elemental, the body spirit, will give people the foundation to be able to do this. As humans work more closely with their body intelligence, they will learn how to travel in space and time and then how to travel at higher frequencies outside of space and time as we dragons can do." [1]

"Okay, I'm curious. How is your way of traveling superior to those of our great human masters?"

"You misunderstand me. Your great masters can travel and manifest as we dragons do, but they didn't demonstrate this to less developed humans. It would have been pointless as no one at a certain stage of evolution could grasp what I'm telling you now.

"Then why speak to me and especially ask me to write about traveling outside of space and time, if it's pointless?" I said, a trifle confrontative.

Jake smiled, indicating that he appreciated me becoming more fiery. Perhaps, this was the way dragons spoke to each other.

"In answer to your excellent question, Jesus lived 2000 years ago and what was true of that time is no longer true now. I'm speaking to you in a world of form that lies beyond the world of form that you would normally know. I'm in my world meditating and contemplating in stillness as I speak with you. You could say that I'm a hologram speaking with you, but that would place what I am in a limited human context.

"My body in the higher astral dragon world has created the form you see in the lower astral human world. My form in my world creates this form to speak with you."

"Whoa," I said. "I need to clarify if the higher and lower astral worlds are the same for you as for me. One of Mahavatar Babaji's greatest disciples, Swami Sri Yukteswar, physically appeared after his death to his disciple, Paramahansa Yogananda, and asked him to write about the various astral worlds in *The Autobiography of a Yogi*. [2]

Sri Yukteswar said, 'There are many astral planets, teeming with astral beings.... Just as many physical suns and stars roam in space, so there are also countless astral solar and stellar systems ... The ordinary astral universe — not the subtler astral heaven of Hiranyaloka (where Sri Yukteswar worked) — is peopled with millions of astral beings who have come, more or less recently, from the Earth, and also with myriads of fairies, mermaids, fishes, animals, goblins, gnomes, demigods and spirits, all residing on different astral planets.'

"That's correct," said Jake. "There are many astral planets existing in various frequencies and dragons live on a planet in a high astral realm close to Hiranyaloka. Beings in our realm are more mental whereas beings in lower realms are more emotional, but both dragons and humans still exist in astral worlds of form."

"So, humans are more governed by their emotions than dragons," I responded.

"Yes. Our mental abilities are more highly evolved and it's not easy to transfer what I know into your human terms."

"I can appreciate that," I said, reminding myself to relinquish sensitivity to what felt like him belittling my and other humans' present state of evolution.

Jake immediately softened his approach in a greater effort to relate. "You might say that our present moment together is beyond space and time. It's not something to think about. It's known. This is a difficult concept for humans who ask questions such as, 'Do you move physically?' 'What do you feel emotionally?' 'What are you thinking about when you travel to other galaxies on these paths of light through deep space'. There is not a better word in human vocabulary for what I'm attempting to convey than to say, as I've said, I and other dragons know this reality. There's no movement. It just is. And in all the crystal cells of our dragon body, we are this reality, even as we are a balance of earth, air, fire, and water."

Jake paused to gauge my reaction and to see if he had addressed his message in a way that was absorbable and desirable.

Quick to reinforce his efforts, I said, "Thanks for clarifying the way that you're able to travel and speak to me and for sharing that human masters can do what you do. This gives me hope for the future as it is something I'd love to do as probably most humans would."

"Good," he replied, relieved. "However, if you agree, I think it's best to stop now to give you time to absorb our discussion. We can continue tomorrow."

"I agree," I replied and exhaled my breath, which I now realized I'd been holding. I was happy to be included in the decision that was increasingly becoming a two-way learning journey.

My Dragon Lineage

Leaving Jake, I returned to my room to wash up for lunch with Prajnaparamita. Lunches and dinners were always with her at which time we shared our lives and our ways of perceiving. She was eager to hear about the dragon and about the various astral realms I walked in while I was eager to understand how an enlightened person perceives our daily world and how it differs from how unenlightened people do. Although we had some different gifts, we were aligned in that both of us were committed to service, teaching, and grounding our work in the Earth.

We were eating lunch when Prajnaparamita broached the topic of the dragon. "Are you able to tell me what the dragon says?" she inquired.

Jake had already requested that, if asked, I only give a summation, so I replied, "It's early days and we're getting to know each other; however, I can tell you a bit. He is the young dragon that was in an egg when I traveled to his world in a vision many decades ago."

"I understand," she said, "but why is it here?"

"I think he's here mostly for me. He has been waiting for a year to speak with me and when the pandits did the fire ceremony, he found a perfect opportunity to come to where I would be."

"Do you think the fire ceremony attracted it?" she inquired, obviously curious about the unsought outcome of conducting fire rituals.

"Dragons love fire and blessed fire is a special treat for them… like chocolate is for us," I said and smiled as we both love chocolate.

"However," I added, "I think he's here mainly for me, but it's strange he would choose to come here instead of to my home in Canada. That said, your temperatures can be higher than 40 C (104 F) degrees in summer, and dragons like heat."

We finished and I was leaving when Prajnaparamita requested, "Let me know if you receive any other information you think would be helpful for me to know."

"Of course," I agreed, walking out the door.

Most of the devotees had been committed to Prajnaparamita for many years. A few were residents, but most had come attracted by the topics I would teach. We were seated in a circle in the orchard and the sun was pleasantly warm after a cool spring. Fortunately, the temperatures were still in the mid-20s Celsius. Unlike my dragon friend, I was not keen on temperatures above 30 Celsius. Healthy apple, pear, chestnut, and birch trees surrounded us and nesting swallows swooped to catch flying insects to feed their chirping youngsters. All in all, an idyllic country setting.

The first day, I had taught about elementals, and, this day, I was teaching about human hybrids. In my book, *Hybrids: So You Think You Are Human*, I discuss the possibility that 22 different races, some from the stars and others from the Earth, have incarnated into our human genome. These I call hybrids. Among these races are elementals, angels, dolphins, and — I guess it's no surprise — dragons.

I knew from Prajnaparamita's reaction a few days before that she didn't want me to discuss the dragon in the forest with the group. Therefore, I spoke only about the characteristics of people who could be dragon hybrids and steered clear of the resident dragon.

"I want to hear more about the dragon living here," one of the participants asked.

Hoping to avoid answering her question, I replied, "The dragon is only one hybrid and it's best to speak about it in the context of the 22 possible hybrids that you and others could be and to do an exercise for you to discover which one you are."

"I'd like to know if there is a dragon here and what it wants," she insisted and this time many other people nodded in agreement.

Ugh! I was caught between the wishes of Prajnaparamita and also the dragon and those of the group. It was not a pleasant experience and there was no way to satisfy everyone.

"I cannot speak about this presently," I said, more assertively.

"Why not?" she demanded, before adding, "Who else would like to know about the dragon who is living here?"

Many more hands went up.

Prajnaparamita was sitting beside me as she was interested in the topics I was teaching. At this point, she ended the debate with, "Not now!"

I was happy that she had closed the discussion. Furthermore, I didn't like to share new information until I had time to process it. I've often noticed that new information, whether it comes from elementals, dragons, or other beings, is raw and I need time to translate it into human terms before it's ready for general consumption.

There were many disappointed faces. Fortunately, after I led them in an exercise to discover their hybrid lineage, they were satisfied once again. After I finished teaching, I went for a quiet walk along the country lane adjoining the property. It's all too easy to sit to teach, sit to meditate, sit for satsang, and sit to speak with the dragon as the day evaporates. Walking in nature allows me time to think of nothing except the beauty of my surroundings. It helps to ground me on the Earth. When I walk, new ideas arise, questions receive answers, and new information is digested. A pause time is essential in my writing and thinking about anything. Even when I'm home working on the computer, I regularly walk around the house and outside, weather permitting, to clear my head. During this pause, many questions that I cannot answer, or decisions that I cannot make, become clear.

Time away from Jake allowed me space to contemplate not only what he had said but also why he had chosen to speak with me.

Yes, I had visited his world in a waking dream, but now I was beginning to wonder if there was a more significant reason that he had sought me. In fact, I was beginning to suspect that I had another reality in the dragon homeworld. Let me explain what I mean.

Jane Roberts, in her book *Oversoul Seven,* many decades ago wrote about how a soul might simultaneously exist in many incarnations. When I originally read Roberts' book, I found myself agreeing with her premise; however, I only saw myself incarnating and being alive at the same time on Earth.

Years later, I extended my view of what was possible when I saw myself on the Pleiades sitting on a mound of what looked like human skulls. I appeared human as if the skulls were the same race as myself, but I had a very stern, non-human look. I was connected with death, like Kali, the Hindu goddess of death.

Another time, in a second waking vision, I saw myself living in an elemental world, not as an elemental, but as a human, a 'wise woman' the elementals called me. Because of these two experiences, it wasn't a stretch to imagine that I had another life in some human-like body in the dragon homeworld and that would explain how I saw myself in a cave with dragons. I can tell the difference between fantasy and true visions and these experiences were definitely of the latter type.

I knew I wouldn't be able to rest until I asked Jake if I had spent time in his world. Because it was the end of the day, John, my dedicated chair mover, would have already taken my chair back to the havan building for the night. Nevertheless, I could still go to the forest and stand while I spoke to Jake.

Turning around, I headed back up the country road and through the meadow towards the forest. Winding my way through the trees, I arrived at the shaded circle where he customarily laired. I stabilized my feet on the ground, closed my two outer eyes, and opened my inner eye. There he was, watching me.

"It's not essential to come here to speak with me," he said, looking a bit perturbed with my interruption. "You can do it as easily on your couch."

"Good to know," I said. "Still, seeing I'm at the ashram where we first began, I thought our connection might be stronger here."

"Perhaps that was true at the beginning when we were first aligning our frequencies, but now any place is a good place as long as you can enter a quiet, calm, and receptive state."

"Because I'm already here, could you answer a question?" I asked before I lost that calm state he required.

"I already know your question and the answer is yes," Jake answered.

Seeing that I wanted no confusion, he added, "That is: yes, you simultaneously live in many worlds and one of these is our dragon world."

He waited patiently for his words to sink in. Meanwhile, faced with this confirmation of my hunch, other questions were arising.

"In the dragon world, I see myself looking human. Is that the way I look to you in your world?"

"Yes and no," he replied curtly.

"I definitely need more information than yes and no," I said, frustrated by his lack of detail. "Yes, to what? No, to what?"

"Very well," he agreed. "I can tell you; however, you could work it out yourself if you didn't doubt your intuition."

"Perhaps that's the case," I granted. "Yet, even if I have an intuition, it's good to have it confirmed…in words, please."

"You have evolved the ability through many lifetimes to travel to various worlds. At first, you came in your imagination and later you developed the ability to live in these worlds."

"How is that possible when these worlds are not made for humans?" I asked, wanting to understand the bits and pieces I'd seen over decades.

"They may not be made for humans physically, but in higher astral frequencies where other worlds exist, you are not physical. If you are relating to yourself with human eyes in my dragon world, then yes, you see yourself in a human body. However, that assumes you have only a human body and that is an erroneous assumption."

"My God," I exclaimed, "this is a lot to take in."

"Of course, it's because you're viewing yourself as an Earth being with a human body," he replied, shaking his head in what I took to be frustration with my sluggish perception.

"I can almost get my head around what you are saying. So," I asked, "if I see myself being a human being in the dragon world, is that the way you dragons see me too?"

"Yes, we see the hologram of the physical human body that you project. However, in higher realities, you can choose any body you wish. You can be a dragon in the dragon world and have another body in another world."

"Is this the way that masters do it?" I inquired curiously.

"Yes and no," Jake replied, asking me to puzzle out what he was saying.

"Bloody hell, not that again," I said, frustrated.

"I'm accurately answering your questions to lead you to the correct answer which, given your preconceptions, you can understand," he said, smirking and satisfied with himself.

"Let me guess," I answered, eager to remove his self-satisfied look. "In higher realms, masters don't need a physical body of any description because they are beings of light energy."

"Right," Jake replied, happy to concede this point. "You know the answer to most of your queries, but you doubt your intuition because it runs counter to how your world views reality, even so-called higher realities. Partially my reason for being with you is to help you remove self-doubt, so you can travel more freely in these higher realities. I recommend that you think of me as your dragon brother. Doing so will assist you to relinquish your restricted view of yourself as only human."

Regarding me with compassionate forbearance, he said, "That's more than enough for today. I'll see you tomorrow. Rest well tonight, sis."

Dismissed, I walked straight back to my room exhausted. There was a lot to absorb and I was beginning to feel that speaking with my dragon brother was raising my frequency. As he had said when we first met, I needed to spiritually stretch, and I was enjoying his exercise in higher learning. I decided to embrace Jake as my dragon brother, as he recommended, to attempt to remove my stuck identification as a human.

Throwbacks on Earth

I was eager to continue my conversation with my dragon brother and fairly skipped through the meadow to the forest the following day. Birds were chirping, and all was right with the world. I entered the woods and made my way briskly to his lair. John had already put my chair in the usual place, so I was set to go. Seating myself, I closed my eyes and was ready for the next installment of the topics Jake wished to cover when the sound of a hedge trimmer broke the peace.

"I'm sure it will stop very soon," I said, hoping I was right. The piercing sound grew louder and closer while I focused unsuccessfully on remaining calm.

Jake had had enough. "It's difficult for you to concentrate with this disruption. You create blocks in your energy to resist the unpleasant sound, rather than flowing in our conversation together."

"I agree, but maybe the noise will end in a minute," I persisted. I was reluctant to ask the person to stop since Prajnaparamita would have asked him to do what he was doing.

"Stop him now," Jake replied fiercely, brooking no denial. "Even if I'm speaking with you as an advanced hologram, it's still disturbing my vibration to endure these unpleasant sounds."

ɔ my feet and quickly went to ask the hedge cutter

ɹad on earmuffs to protect his ears and didn't hear my

ɹ. Sure enough, he was one of the people in my course who

ɹ   ɹnown an interest in dragons. I had to stand directly in front of him before he noticed me. Taking off his ear protectors, he waited for me to speak.

"I'm meditating in the forest, William," I said. "If you could work somewhere else, I'd appreciate it."

Nodding his head in agreement and notably not asking about why I was in the area reserved for the dragon, he left. Grateful for his cooperation, and taking time to restore my inner calm, I slowly walked back to Jake.

"We aren't a technological race," he began before I could say a word. "This is not the line along which we've developed. Being a blending of four elements — and even more elements that you don't know yet — we're able to do everything that you would do by using technology through the alignment of our essence with the Source of All.

"I'd like to hear more about your world," I asked, hoping he'd comply.

"Our world, which you will visit soon, has wonderful lakes, mountains, crystals, and minerals. Our senses are nurtured and fed by pleasant sounds and vistas."

"Elementals have told me that they're able to take the essence of food that humans give them. Are your senses fed by sound and lovely environments?" I asked curiously.

"We're beings of great power and longevity and we feed our senses with pleasantness, even as you feed yourself physical food. Humans believe dragons are carnivores that want to eat livestock and deer and this is ridiculous. It's far beneath where we are in evolution."

"Then why do our human stories speak about dragons doing this?" I inquired, confused.

"I'll explain," Jake said. "In earlier times, some dragons came to your world that were, in your terms, laggards. We're born … Hmmm … perfect. However, some were not completely perfect and needed more discipline. They were throwbacks on the path of dragon evolution. You could say they were crippled or underdeveloped. Sometimes when this occurs, we send throwbacks to lower frequencies where they can stabilize and heal, rather than attempt to help them in the frequency in which we dragons live."

I had a hunch about which lower-frequency location he was thinking of and was not pleased. He, of course, heard my thoughts.

"Let me give you an example to which you might relate," he said in an apologetic tone. "Consider how impossible it would be for a person in grade one in your school system to take a university course. When one of ours is in grade one, we take them to planets with a lower frequency where they can learn to stabilize. When they go to a lower frequency, they cannot live on the essence of their senses because the frequency is too low to feed them. Therefore, they need to make do with whatever is available."

"Is this why they ate deer and cattle and sometimes humans on Earth?" I asked, not willing to accept what the dragons had done.

"Don't rush ahead and misinterpret what I'm saying," Jake said, giving me a scolding look. "This is why your myths about dragons speak of them wanting to find jewels and crystals to take to their lairs. The throwbacks went to caves where there were crystals and semi-precious gems because the energy was strongest there for them to rest and sleep. In crystal caves, they were able to sleep for eons in a semi-awake state learning to stabilize. When this was happening, they didn't need to eat because they were absorbing the essence from these crystals and gems."

"I seem to remember something about dragons wanting gold, too. Is this the case?" I asked.

"It's true because gold is the metal that holds the highest frequency on Earth."

"I think I understand. So what humans see as coveting is actually food for dragons?"

"Exactly," Jake replied. "If dragons were disturbed in their lairs where this food was available, they had to resort to cattle and sheep to give themselves at least some nourishment."

I noticed that he conveniently left out the eating of humans, but I decided not to prod him with questions about this. Too late, he picked up my fleeting thought and responded.

"The throwbacks preferred not to be around humans because humans hunted them while they were undergoing their healing process. What's more, humans valued crystals, gems, and gold and misunderstood the dragon's motivation for wanting these things. If the dragons were greatly disturbed, they might become insane and then resort to unpleasant behavior against the humans."

"I appreciate you explaining the deeper realities behind our human myths about dragons. It helps me to feel more compassion for dragons that have come to our planet."

My dragon brother paused for a moment and I felt him weighing what next to say. I was starting to pick up the subtle gestures he used when he was thinking, and I noticed that his feathery eyebrows began to wave ... a sure sign of him trying to decide what to say to me. Coming to a decision, he continued, "There were a few among you who could converse with dragons even in their fallen state. Most assuredly in their fallen state because healthy dragons, coming from a high frequency world, would feel themselves superior to humans and have no desire to communicate with you. Because of their developmental delays, the throwbacks felt separated from the Source of All and other dragons. Most didn't want to further lower their frequency by speaking with humans, but a few did. Do you have any questions?"

Jake raised his right eyebrow and looked meaningfully at me, inviting me to ask a question. I found it odd that he didn't tell me what he wanted to say and, instead, sent me on a guessing game.

"Please say more about throwbacks that did speak with humans?" I inquired, hoping that I was asking the right question. He smiled in amused tolerance and I realized that puzzles were part of the teaching technique used by dragons and that I'd solved this one and had won the prize of his answer.

"Over thousands of years, a small number of throwbacks talked with humans. You could almost say befriended, but that would not be the right word. They did this because they were lonely and humans were the closest thing to being sentient like them. Besides, they had lost the ability to increase their frequency to a high enough level to return to our dragon world. These throwbacks realized that they would be forever separated from us, so a few of them did speak with humans. This communication depended on many things including the consciousness and interest of the human, environment in which the human lived, and the motivation of the dragon.

"In a previous life, you were one of these humans," my dragon brother said. "Because of this, our frequencies are in better alignment than if you and I had to align with each other from scratch. Your past life experience with a dragon makes it easier for us to communicate and to better understand each other."

"I can't say I'm surprised by this revelation," I answered. "I've suspected that hundreds of years ago I had an Asian life, probably Chinese, where I spoke with a dragon. I've seen myself as a man in beautiful silk robes and had a feeling that I was a scholar. Is that the life to which you refer?"

"It is," he replied and smiled at me indulgently as if he were the proud older brother to a younger sibling.

"However, there is something I find confusing," I said, wanting clarification. "You mentioned that the dragons on Earth were all throwbacks and I don't feel that I was speaking to an insane, unstable being who was in danger of killing me. Why is that?"

My dragon friend threw back his head and began laughing. Intrigued by why he found my question so amusing, I waited patiently.

Still smiling broadly, Jake focused his eyes on me and said, "Humans have care workers who look after individuals with disabilities; we dragons have our equivalent of the same thing. Our care workers occasionally came to the Earth to check on the throwbacks to ascertain if any had progressed enough to return to our dragon world. Our care workers carried crystals holding higher curative frequencies both to give to the throwbacks and to place in their caves. This was to assist the throwbacks to raise their frequencies."

"Did I speak with a care worker?" I asked, hoping that I had.

"Dragons are curious by nature," he replied, deflecting my question. "One care worker who, by the way, is of a special lineage, while seeking to do her work, looked around for the best environments to help the throwbacks. The Chinese civilization at that time was more advanced and at a higher frequency than Europe. Therefore, the care worker suggested to the more advanced throwbacks that they dwell in China and other Asian countries. One of these more advanced throwbacks chose to speak with you."

"I don't know if I should be flattered or insulted," I said. "It doesn't seem to me that a mentally ill dragon spoke to me. In what way was he a throwback and how do you even know this?"

"The memories of every dragon and their history are kept by us," Jake replied. "The care workers have responsibility to carry the history of the throwbacks back to our world. We need this information to decide with whom we wish to breed and which qualities we wish and which ones we don't."

"I see. So, in answer to my other question, in what way was the dragon with whom I spoke a throwback?"

"Let's start with his strength, shall we?" said Jake, rhetorically.

"The dragon who spoke with you was a scholar and belonged to that lineage among us. He was attracted to you because you, too, were a scholar. And by sharing his knowledge of dragons, he hoped to preserve these desirable qualities both in himself and in your world. He taught you about these positive qualities and, in the Asian world, you helped to establish the message that dragons were powerful allies. Because dragons are long-lived, he knew that he had succeeded in his task and this kept him sane and stable. Furthermore, the fact that emperors aligned themselves with dragons fed his pride and self-esteem. These are all desirable qualities for dragons."

"I'm grateful to know that I helped stabilize at least one dragon and kept dragons from being hated in Asia like they were hated in Europe. But I'd still like to know in what way he was a throwback?"

"I was coming to that," huffed my dragon brother and I could tell that my continual questions were wearing on him. "He was too emotional."

"Emotional," I countered. "What emotions are unacceptable to dragons? Oh, let me guess, it's anger, isn't it?"

"Why would you choose anger?" Jake asked, intrigued by my insight.

"I have a vague memory of the dragon who spoke with me having a bad temper and that I had to be careful not to say anything that would upset him. He was unpredictable and frightening if he was angry."

"You are correct. That was his problem," he replied. "It surprises me that you recall this. Very dragon-like to have such an incredible memory of your past lives."

"I'd like to hear…" I started, but he cut me off.

"That's enough for today. We'll see you tomorrow," he said and disappeared.

I arose from the chair and ambled back through the forest and meadow to my little abode. I was happy to have a short break before lunch and my afternoon session. I thoroughly enjoyed the balance of time alone with my dragon brother, time enjoying lunch with Prajnaparamita, and time teaching the group. Today's topic was to be the body elemental, the consciousness within our body, the body spirit.

After a leisurely lunch with Prajnaparamita, I made my way to the orchard and was introducing the topic when John interrupted, "Could we do something to work with the trees? They're suffering with the hot summers and lack of rain, and I feel connected to them."

Letting my eyes drift around the group, I said, "We can do this if people would rather concentrate on healing the trees, but then we won't have time to work with your body elemental. Could we have a show of hands of those who prefer to work with the trees?"

Most of their hands went up, so I quickly agreed, "Okay, trees it is."

Not being able to give them the information they sought the previous day about the dragon, I was more than happy to go with their first choice now.

"When we did the exercise yesterday on hybrids," I asked, "did anyone discover that you were either a forest elf or tree deva? Both of these hybrids have a strong connection to trees."

At least a quarter of the group members raised their hands, which was more than I usually saw in hybrid workshops. I noticed that one of these was John and another was William who had been cutting the hedge that morning.

"Could we work with the trees in the orchard," asked Sam, another forest elf.

All my work is participatory, so I led the group members in an exercise to find the tree in the orchard that wished to speak with them. Folks often ask me how I'm able to speak with beings in other dimensions and I teach many ways to do this. However, by far, the best way is to help others trust their intuition that they, themselves, can speak with trees, elementals, and other beings.

After the group dispersed to find their trees, I turned to Prajnaparamita who was seated beside me. "Don't you want to find the tree who wishes to speak with you?" I inquired.

Casting her eyes above where we sat, I saw the limbs of a willow swaying in the breeze. "I am sitting with the tree that speaks to me," she answered, beaming with her warm smile.

Looking around at which person had chosen which tree, I noticed that no one had chosen the giant chestnut to our left. "It's interesting," I remarked to Prajnaparamita, "that no one has gone to the chestnut, especially when it's so cool in its shade. Instead, almost everyone has chosen smaller fruit trees in the hot sun."

"It's not surprising to me," she answered. "We eat the fruit from those fruit trees and some of them have been planted by these people; therefore, they feel more connected to those trees."

"I understand what you mean. When we plant something and eat its fruits, there is a stronger connection."

"Everyone takes his or her turn working in the vegetable garden, cutting wood, or planting trees, so they feel connected to this land," Prajnaparamita said.

"It's wonderful what you're doing," I responded. "It's a disease in our Western world that people are not rooted on the earth. They move from house to house, job to job, place to place, and, lacking roots in the land, they don't mind destroying it. I believe this is what has caused our alienation from Mother Earth that has led to our environmental crisis."

We continued our discussion until others returned to share their experiences. It was clear that their connection with both one tree and the entire orchard had deepened through talking directly with their chosen tree. What they said led me to think that, if each of us took time daily to speak with plant, tree, and animal beings, we'd realize that all beings on Earth are our brothers and sisters. And, by extension, what my dragon brother was teaching me was that we humans are connected to beings not only on Earth but throughout the cosmos.

The Source of All

I greeted the day with gratitude. How fortunate I was to be in such a peaceful environment walking to my usual place in the forest. Arriving, I waited calmly for Jake to acknowledge my presence. While waiting, I moved into deeper and deeper meditation. Turning my attention to where he usually rested, I became aware that his aura seemed larger and fuller than it had been previously.

My dragon brother greeted me. "We wanted you in this deeply receptive state because then your rhythms and breathing are almost as slow as ours. Our metabolism is slow to conserve energy and to be receptive to infusion by the Source of All. You would call this infusion 'prana', but we call it merging. We surrender to being infused. Being embraced. Being.

"When we're young, we don't do this as much," Jake continued. "The older we become, the more deeply we rest and surrender to the depths of the embrace. Merging. And in this deep state, we come to know All. All.

As he spoke, I remained in the same deeply receptive state that he was describing. I had no desire to speak and was completely open to whatever he wished to say. No longer did I feel a need to carry on a conversation as our relationship had entered a comfortable place of acceptance of each other.

"Dragons have many lineages. Many jeweled, colored rays. Indigo dragons are wisdom keepers. Our wisdom streams from this deep merging and, when we are infused by the Source of All, each crystalline cell in our body receives a drop of wisdom and we are full. Then we digest for long periods. Resting. You would say that we are in bliss; however, we don't have a word for it. It's a … Hmmm … Hmmm.

"Your human throat cannot produce it," Jake said when I attempted to replicate the sound. "Even as the bees hum with the soul's frequency, we hum with the Source of All. Our hum resonates through all the crystalline drops of being, tuning us slowly. And, as we age, each crystalline drop grows larger filling us more and more until all of these crystalline structures merge. We lose the desire to do anything but to stay, like this, not moving. Resonating with the Source of All. Our old ones, our sacred ones, do this.

"Younger dragons," Jake carried on, "sit with the old ones where — aligned with them — the younger ones are fed with the older ones' resonating wisdom."

As he spoke, his dragon essence poured over me. I harmonized with what he was describing as if I, too, was in the presence of an old dragon. I didn't feel like speaking; however, a question arose lightly in my thoughts.

"You ask," he said, answering my whispered thought, "if the old indigo dragons resonate on all rays like the Source of All?"

"We dragons are beings on one stream. The Source of All is on all streams. We can be touched by all streams. We can merge much deeper than you currently know with your human-limited consciousness.

But we still have this dragon form, this filter to receive the Source of All. In this way, we are one with and fed by the Source of All. An old one has come to sit with you today so that you can merge with us."

"Ahh," I thought to myself. "He has brought one of these old ones. That is the large presence I have been feeling."

"You are only able to receive a little of this resonance from our wise one, but you do obtain some," Jake said. "You, by your very nature, are restless and disturb the harmony. Other young dragons wouldn't want to sit with you because they would be disturbed when they aligned themselves with our wise one. Merging, merging, merging in this grid of light."

"Say more about the grid of light?" I thought quietly as I didn't want to disturb my calm state.

"There are wise ones in every dragon lineage and they are linked in a grid to create a jewel of memory. You cannot see this form and, even for us, it's in higher frequencies. A crystal note exists at a very high frequency and it's created by the old ones of our dragon lineages. They feed this crystal — which is not the same way you think of crystal. You could say it's the storage of our power, wisdom, and knowing."

I must have had a gap in my understanding that Jake sought to fill because he added, "You have books. We have this. It is from this crystal being that I have been formed by way of my mother and father. We would say dam and sire. The knowing of what I was to be, what I would serve, came from them listening to this crystal jewel of memory."

From my deep meditative state, I spoke to my dragon brother, "I believe that through transmuting the pressures brought from our environment, and with deep yearning, and by surrendering our individual identity, we can turn the coal of our limited ego state into a diamond body. This diamond body is the enlightened state of merging that you describe."

"Yes, this is the equivalent of what I am describing," he agreed. "This crystal, which has been built by our ancestors and old wise ones, maintains the harmony of our world. It is aligned with the Source of All and its energy beams down on us, keeping us in harmony with the Source."

I thought Jake was going to finish speaking, but he took a deep breath and continued along a different vein. "Your Sun is evolving. It will ultimately collapse in on itself and become a black hole. During that process, it is surrendering and cocooning. Its fire doesn't burn out. Instead, the Sun rebirths itself like a phoenix again and again. Your Sun is powered by the Source of All that you refer to as the Great Central Sun, or the Galactic Center. Suns go into a cocooning stage, which to you looks like a collapse. This is a transmutation process for the Sun to be reborn in higher dimensions in a crystalline form."

I was intrigued that Jake wished to speak about our Sun, but I wasn't certain why he was addressing this topic.

I whispered, "This is interesting about our Sun; however, what does this have to do with human and dragon evolutions?"

"It's rare that humans can see, even vaguely, what we are describing," he answered. "We are speaking of what is occurring in the 12th dimension, which is a much higher frequency than you are capable of maintaining.

"And does it end there?" Jake asked rhetorically. "We don't know. The question, 'Where are we going?' occasionally arises among us young ones. The old wise ones don't ask this and don't care because they are merged with the Source of All. But we young ones are restless, curious, and hungry for knowing. We are eager to take the next step to transcend what a dragon is presently. All beings seek to transcend their current level of consciousness. Each galaxy has one great being, one great Creator and our Source of All evolves as well. Furthermore, there are others beyond our Creator. That is enough for now."

Not ready to stop, I pulled out of my meditative state. "I'm grateful that you asked an old one to sit with me, so I could rest in the energy."

"Actually, I took you with me to be with the old one in our dragon world," Jake replied. "I wanted you to have an experience similar to what we have with our wise ones."

"It was amazing and I could feel the great difference in depth and energy between you and the old one," I acknowledged. "It's incredible that you could take me to your world. How do you do it?"

"You and I have created a magnetic harmonic cord between us that allows me to bring you to the old one. However, it's not easy for you to maintain this coherent state. To do so, you must hold yourself alert at the same time as being non-attached to either being or doing anything — which is the ego state — and this state feels to you almost like the pre-sleep state. This extended pause in the eternal present is enlightenment. Enlightenment, self-realization, is none other than what you view as an extended pause."

"Are you certain this is enlightenment?" I queried. "I was still conscious, but deeply receptive. I suppose you could say surrendered."

"It is the same. Realize that you are in the right place at the right time to speak with me. There is nothing else to say. Nothing more for today. Just be here surrendered in the energy."

I continued sitting quietly and, once again, entered a deeply meditative state. I am not certain when Jake withdrew as he was no longer present when I emerged from meditation. I found it intriguing that as a hologram he could either be with me or remove himself. It would be a good question to ask him tomorrow.

Stiff from having sat so long and feeling more than full from our conversation, I slowly arose from the chair and meandered back to my room. Looking longingly at the bed, then at the clock, reality entered. It was time to teach.

It was hot... around 30 C degrees. I'm not great in the heat and tend to wilt. This afternoon, I would be taking the group around the property to discover what nature wanted to say to them. This would assist them to be better caretakers of the land. Unhurriedly and in silence, we set out through the vegetable garden and, although we were going to the same place, I noticed that some followed the path and others chose to walk on the grass beside the path. I chose the path and when we got to the first stop, the food forest, I asked the others, "Why did you choose to walk either on the grass or on the path?"

"It's easier walking on the path," said Doris.

That had been my reason as well. It's always easier to follow an existing path than to create a new one yourself.

"And you?" I asked John who hadn't been following the path.

"I prefer the grass," he said simply. John never used two words when one would do.

The food forest is a semi-wild area in the meadow where they grow different species of edible plants. Walking silently, each of us chose a plant, bush, or tree that called to us. Many would have preferred that I tell them what each plant communicated to me, but that is not my way. At the ashram each person takes turns weeding, planting, and watering the food forest; therefore, I thought it was essential that everyone learn to communicate and have faith in their communication with the plants and land. After all, they were eating the fruits of these plants, so it was important to nurture these relationships.

Being in the glaring sun was enough to finish off a third of the group who retreated to the comfort of shade back at the house. I envied them and was happy that our next stop was the beehives on the shaded edge of the forest. The devotees had built three beehives earlier that spring, but all remained empty. Because no bees arrived, Prajnaparamita had requested that we invite them to come.

Together we gathered around one of the hives and I proceeded to lead the group in a meditation to call the bees to the new hive. There was a hive of wild bees in a tree near where the dragon dwelled and I focused my attention on those bees to ask them to send a new queen.

"Imagine," I said to the group members, "that you see a queen bee coming to your new hive. Imagine her being happy. See the worker bees going to your food forest to fertilize your plants and bushes. Bees hum with the sound of the soul, so hear that sound."

We continued our meditation for some time and had just finished when Dana arrived from the main house saying, "You've got to come back, immediately."

"Why?" I asked, being reluctant to end our meditative journey around the property.

"A poisonous viper was found in the vegetable garden," Dana answered. This was not great news given that we had walked through that garden on the way to the food forest.

Hastening to comply, we walked briskly back to the main house where Prajnaparamita waited. "We've called the fire department to remove the snake," she said.

"Have you ever had a viper here before," I asked, thinking it might be best to no longer wear sandals.

"Not inside our enclosed orchard and houses, although we know they're in the forest," Prajnaparamita replied.

Her answer didn't reassure me as I imagined what could happen on my lone daily treks to my dragon brother.

"Has anyone ever been bitten by a viper?" I asked, wanting to set my mind at rest.

"No," she smiled. "They are not aggressive but we have children playing in the orchard that we want to protect."

"And, if anyone were bitten, how serious would it be?" I inquired, hopefully.

"Very serious," she said, "but the firemen are trained in this and would be here within minutes."

At that moment, Dana returned from dealing with the firemen. "They've taken the snake away."

"What are they going to do with it?" was our immediate question as, viper or not, none of us supported killing the snake.

"They'll release it in a forest away from people," Dana responded, reassuring us.

The group broke up and we went our own ways. I was left to consider if there was a relationship between the viper coming into our enclosed courtyard and the dragon. I've read stories wherein a dragon is often referred to as a snake.

This would be my first question the next morning when I would speak with Jake. Meanwhile, I returned to my room to change from sandals into hiking boots.

The Snake and the Dragon

The following day, hiking boots laced tightly, I set off for the forest. I walked firmly and was careful to stay on the path and out of the long grass. Snakes hear vibration and I created as much vibration as possible to give any snake a chance to avoid me. I was not at ease and, whereas yesterday I'd felt safe in a known environment, now I was cautious. At the same time, I was aware of my overreaction to the snake incident. The ashram had been going for 12 years and no one had been bitten, so there was little likelihood this would change. Still, I couldn't help but think that I had attracted the viper, not consciously, but with my energy and that of the dragon.

Arriving at the lair of my dragon brother, I sat down in my chair and closed my eyes. He was waiting so I got straight to the point. "Has your presence drawn the viper from the forest inside the walled orchard?"

"The snake is our relative, as the chimpanzee is yours," Jake replied. "Even as the Tuatha de Danaan are the ancestors of the elementals, we dragons are the ancestors of the snakes."

"Prajnaparamita asked why you chose this place as she is concerned for the safety of her people?" I said.

"There are several reasons. The fire energy of the havan and the high frequency of the meditations, ceremonies, and working in a meditative mode, attracts me. Also, I knew you were coming and I prepared to meet you."

"And what is the relationship between you, me, and the snakes?" I asked firmly.

"We dragons are old wise ones and snakes are our children. As far as you, me, and snakes are concerned, I'd remind you that energy flows through the two snake-like channels that connect the chakras in your body. When the energy between these two channels is equal and unblocked, it merges and moves up your central channel into self-realization... enlightenment."

"I confess," I said, "I had not related you and snakes to my kundalini energy although I had considered that the havan ceremony might have attracted you."

"Let me continue," said Jake. "You need to remember that snakes and dragons have been sacred in many cultures prior to Christianity. The Celts believed that dragons were akin to gods. They associated them with power, fertility, and wisdom. Druids believed that they were the gatekeepers to other worlds and that the dragon world existed parallel to the human world."

"How is it that you know our human history in such detail?" I asked, impressed by his knowledge.

"That's easy," he said grinning and obviously proud of his accomplishment. "As I mentioned before, I can read all your knowledge and memories as easily as you read a book. Likewise, I can read the collective memories of humanity in the ethers. For example, I know that the Oracle at Delphi in ancient Greece was called the Python and that the pharaohs of Egypt wore a headdress with a snake emerging above their third eye indicating enlightenment.

"Very well," I acknowledged. "I get it. Snakes in ancient cultures were sacred and associated with spiritual consciousness. But what do we do about the snakes here?"

"The snakes, our children, are attracted by meditation and by the yearning for enlightenment among you and others here. Chanting, prayers, and devotion urge the kundalini energy to rise through the snake-like channels within you. In the same way, these practices attract physical snakes to places where this energy resides. This is not to blame or accuse, but to clarify that what happens in the spiritual frequency also happens in the physical."

"Yes, but the snakes here are poisonous…"

"So was the cobra for the pharaohs," Jake interrupted.

I shrugged indicating that I remained unconvinced by his argument. He continued, "In India, snake charmers play the flute and the cobras rise listening to the music. The cobra does not feel challenged, but rather comforted through beautiful music with which the cobra is in harmony."

"Great in theory," I granted, "however, not being professional snake charmers, what do we do with these snakes? Do we continue to call the fire brigade to take them away? Do we capture them ourselves to take them to the forest? Or do we live with them?"

"There's a larger question," he said, showing that he was trying to solve the dilemma that concerned us humans. "Because my energy attracts the snakes, Prajnaparamita must choose whether I stay or leave. I can leave when you do, or I can create another high-frequency hologram to remain here. If I remain, I wish to be left alone and only disturbed once every few months to be given ashes from a havan ceremony."

"If I leave, the snakes won't be as interested in staying," he said. "However, Tanis, you are also a focus of snake energy here. It's not a coincidence that the snakes come inside the enclosed orchard closer to you. It's good for everyone that you have rooted to this land; yet, I recommend that you remove your etheric energy when you leave. By doing this, snakes won't be attracted to the orchard."

"I want to share what you have said with Prajnaparamita and I'll speak with you tomorrow," I said, getting to my feet to leave. "Tomorrow is Pentecost, which is an important day for me because so many incredible things have happened on that day. A friend is coming to join me for Pentecost and I'd like to get ready for his arrival."

I left the forest and walked swiftly back towards my room. Coming around the corner of a building about 25 feet from my door, I met two people intently staring at a wall. One of these was Denis, a man who works at the ashram full-time. The other was Marianne who had been pruning flowers nearby when I left.

"What's happening," I asked, intrigued. "What are you looking at?"

"I found another viper, a small one, and it's curled around that pipe," Marianne answered, pointing.

Sure enough, there it was: Viper number two. The baby viper looked harmless and scared. "What are you going to do?" I asked, hoping for a good solution.

"I'm trying to capture it," Denis said. Working with a spade, he was busy removing the stones around the little snake.

The fire brigade came and, when they arrived, Denis gave the small viper to them to remove from the property. I returned to my room thinking about the baby viper. Clearly, a large mother viper was somewhere nearby, and most likely other little vipers, too. Lunch would be soon, but I had time to meditate and remove any of my energy that might be attracting the snakes.

During our meal, Prajnaparamita, not surprisingly, asked, "Do you think the dragon is attracting the snakes?"

"Yes," I replied, "as are the fire ceremonies and the spiritual nature of the meditation and ceremonies you are doing here. Snakes find this high spiritual energy attractive. Also, the fact that the dragon is talking to me daily draws the snakes. I think it will be better when I leave. A hologram of the dragon can stay here, or, if you prefer, you can ask him to leave. It's your decision."

Noticing Prajnaparamita's interest in what I was saying, I offered, "I've recorded the conversations with the dragon and, if you want, I can play what the dragon said today. I translate into English what I telepathically hear him say."

"Yes, I'd like that," she replied, rising from her chair and asking at the same time, "Would you like some tea?"

We moved to the sofa and, while drinking our tea, I played the section I'd recorded on my iPhone that day. "It's very raw," I explained. "I telepathically receive a great deal of knowing in my body and memory that is not recorded on my cell phone. Because of this, I never play raw footage for others, but I'm happy to make an exception so you can hear, at least partially, what the dragon said."

I started the recording and Prajnaparamita leaned over, fascinated by what she heard. We paused it many times to discuss various things the dragon said. It was a new experience for me to share information so early in the process of having received it. As soon as the recording finished, we looked at the clock and knew it was time to go to the orchard for my teaching.

"You go ahead," she said.

I left and was waiting with the group when Prajnaparamita arrived carrying a small parcel. "I have a gift for you," she smiled, handing me a beautiful pink bag covered with gold embroidered roses.

Holding the bag and, without undoing the string, I felt a hard oval object inside. "I have a feeling I know what this is," I said to her, pleased. "Shall I open it?"

"If you like," she invited, beaming.

Putting my hand inside the bag, I withdrew a lovely crystal egg wrapped in hand-painted silk.

"Thank you so much. I'll put it on my altar when I get home."

We both knew that the egg represented my work with the dragon. What a wonderful gift and blessing to receive from her.

"But that's not all," Prajnaparamita said, waving her hand to include the others, who were smiling. "They have been practicing a *Grandmother's Healing Haka* which we learned from a Maori medicine man when we visited New Zealand and they are ready to perform it to thank you for coming."

"Fantastic," I said, excited. Every morning I'd heard Maori chanting in the courtyard outside my window, but the group had asked me not to look and I'd complied, knowing they wanted to surprise me with something special… and I love gifts. Doesn't everyone?

All of us moved to a place in the orchard where they could move freely. Men lined up on one side and women lined up on the other side facing the men. Together the men danced forward towards the woman chanting a 'haka'. Then they receded like the waves of the ocean followed by the women dancing in tandem towards the men chanting. It was absolutely beautiful, uplifting, and inspiring. It's amazing what Prajnaparamita has created in only 12 years. Healthy orchards and gardens, profound meditations, and music. Her ashram is full and rich — both physically and spiritually.

After the haka, I left to welcome my friend, Christoph. I'd told Prajnaparamita about his work with farmers and bees and I was happy that she had invited him to dinner.

We were enjoying our meal when Prajnaparamita asked him, "Tell me about your work."

Christoph replied, "I am diverse in terms of my farmer training and practical experience. On one farm I worked with horses, on another I pruned grape vines, and on another, looked after fruit trees. I have years of experience in many areas of plant cultivation and raising animals. I also came to understand and master modern agricultural technology. Some of my work has been to fill in for farmers who needed a holiday and I was fortunate to travel throughout the Black Forest area to work on different kinds of farms. I've had many intensive experiences with farmers, which has given me a diverse and positive understanding of this profession. This has helped in my current business of helping to build contacts and relationships between small farmers and consumers."

Prajnaparamita listened intently. After she finished speaking, she asked, "I know you've driven from Germany today, but if you're not too tired, I'd like to take you on a tour of the property. We've put in three new beehives and I'd like to hear what you have to say about attracting bees to them."

"I'd be happy to assist," Christoph answered, rising from his chair. Christoph is always willing to help others and when that entails helping others with farming, he's doubly keen.

Prajnaparamita invited her devotees to join us and together we set out on a tour. Dusk was approaching when we finally came to the empty beehives. Christoph went closer to inspect the hives and, eager to hear any wisdom he had about beekeeping, the group members surrounded him.

Christoph realized that none of them had experience with bee-keeping, so he kept his talk general. "Our honeybee is a domestic animal and it is important to learn about the animal," he said. "What is its life cycle? What does it need to be healthy? How does it get through the winter?"

He also spoke about the varroa mite which is causing great damage to bees in Europe. The group listened attentively. Although I'd given spiritual meditative assistance to them to attract the bees, he provided practical, concrete advice which they gobbled up. Hopefully, the bees would soon come.

The sun was setting and it was getting dark when we turned for home. It had been a very full day. I retired to my room almost immediately, so that I'd be rested for Pentecost in the morning and Christoph, tired from his long drive from Germany, did the same.

Pentecost, Kundalini, and Babaji

Prajnaparamita, being oriented more to Buddhist and Hindu practices, does not observe Pentecost as a special day. I, however, feel a strong connection to the Christian tradition and Pentecost is important to me. Pentecost, if you are unfamiliar with the term, is when the fire of the Holy Spirit descended on the heads of Jesus' disciples and they became enlightened. I've experienced many unexpected and amazing encounters with fire on that day and one of the most dramatic ones occurred at a retreat led over 30 years ago by Jean Houston, an American author and thought leader involved in the human potential movement.

It was the evening of Pentecost and 60 participants in the retreat were silently walking in single file through a labyrinth in the dark. Each of us held a lit candle and I was deeply praying when the woman walking behind me suddenly began to hit me on top of my head yelling, "Fire! She's on fire!" Within seconds, people came running. They encircled me and continued to brush scorched hair from the top of my head. The woman, naturally upset and flustered about what had occurred, told the onlookers, "I was walking behind her and the flame from my candle actually leapt onto the top of her head." I, too, was dazed by what had happened and didn't know what to make of the experience when a kind bystander gave me her mirror and I surveyed the damage. Sure enough, there was a large bald spot exactly where a monk's tonsure would be.

Now, three decades later, I'm in France and I hoped my dragon brother could shed light on what this and my other Pentecostal experiences with fire meant. It was my last day at the ashram, so, after breakfast, I left Christoph to wander the property by himself and went alone to speak with Jake.

Jake wasted no time before he addressed my as-yet-unspoken question. "You have had so many fire experiences on Pentecost is because of your dragon lineage from both your human mother and father. Your human mother carried the water dragon lineage and your human father was a fire dragon. Moreover, your sire and mine in the dragon world is a ruby dragon."

I'd come to think of Jake as an indigo dragon, so I must have looked perplexed because he volunteered. "Yes, you're correct, I am mainly of the indigo lineage, but I have ruby undertones through our sire. Your human father had both the indigo and ruby lineages, too. Our indigo lineage can catalyze the energy that is needed for spiritual transformation to connect with the Source of All and the ruby lineage adds more power to this process. You have received fire dragon energy from both your human and dragon parents."

"Stop! I have some questions," I interrupted, overwhelmed by what he was saying. "I am a human, so how can I have a dragon sire and how can this be the same as yours? You've called me your nest sister and spoken about our brood mother. It is physically difficult for me to accept what you're saying, although metaphorically I accept that you are my dragon brother and friend on the spiritual path. In this way, I regard my relationship with you as an honor."

"I realize that you currently view yourself as a human and that you have difficulty fully accepting your dragon lineage, but a time will come when you will recognize this. Meanwhile, postpone judgment and stay open to the possibility that you are my nest sister and that we have the same mother and sire in the dragon world."

"Okay. I'll try," I agreed in principle that Jake and I might have the same dragon sire — whatever that meant — but he was pushing me too far in accepting that my human father also had dragon lineage. How could this be possible?

"I have another question. How is my human father of the same indigo and ruby dragon lineage as yours?"

"I am speaking about soul, not personality lineages, and soul lineages are the same in all worlds. You'll have to spiritually expand to understand what I'm going to tell you now: Your father in the human world is related to your sire in the dragon world, so he and I are related, too."

"Oh my God," I replied, overwhelmed. "This is quite a stretch. I need some time to contemplate what you're saying."

"I know," Jake replied. "Don't rush anything and let all come to you with ease."

While I focused on relaxing and letting go of my need-to-know answers before they were ready to be known, Jake said, "I'd like to discuss how dragons ignite the energy in the human body. Yesterday, I spoke about snakes and their relationship with the kundalini energy in your body. This snake or dragon-like energy winds through your seven chakras to catalyze enlightenment."

"Stop. What has this got to do with dragons?" I realized that I was sounding argumentative, but there were too many leaps and twists in the information he was asking me to consume and I was getting a bad case of indigestion. He picked up on what he considered to be my problem but decided to humor me by backtracking and speaking simply.

"We dragons work with the Source of All, the Holy Spirit you would say, to catalyze this energy that moves through your chakras. It would be helpful to understand the stages through which humanity has evolved, and what needs to be done now.

"There are developmental points in humanity along the ascending path through the chakras. Firstly, Spirit must catalyze the energy in the root chakra which is connected to the physical body and the Earth. After you have learned how to ground yourself in your physical body, the energy moves to the second chakra — that of personal relationships. Once you learn to have positive personal relationships, the energy moves to the third chakra, the solar plexus. In this chakra, you are concerned with manifesting your identity. What is your gift to the world, to others, to yourself?

From there, the energy moves to the heart. After you have discovered your gift, it is time to give it to others in service. In your heart chakra, you move from self-service to service for others. This is currently where humanity must focus. There's no sense talking about the higher chakras because we want to focus on the fire in your heart. This is what the dragons in our lineage are concerned with catalyzing in you at this moment."

"Hold on!" I interrupted before he could continue. I was aware that I was being defensive; however, I resisted what he was saying for several reasons, one of these being that the path I followed emphasized the importance of the third eye — which Jake was ignoring.

"Paramahansa Yogananda and the lineage to whom he belongs," I said, "which, by the way, includes Mahavatar Babaji who recommended I speak with dragons, says the focus in meditation must be on the third eye, the sixth chakra, which is the path back to the Source of All. There appears to be a discrepancy between their instructions and yours."

"You," Jake answered, looking at me with strained patience, "have quite an open third eye, which gives you strength in intuition, but you and humanity need to develop the heart. There must be no separation, no boundaries in your thoughts and feelings between yourself and others. This is the time of merging with others. This is the time of global awareness. All countries will merge into one...one humanity. This is our message on Pentecost, not only for you but also for others. We dragons light the fire of service in your heart and on your planet. There is to be no 'other', no undesirable, no preferred. All beings are YOU."

I had to admit that his answer made sense, but I wasn't totally convinced and some dangling ideas still needed to be tied up for me to accept everything he said. "I have never given any thought to dragons working with my kundalini energy and, to tell you the truth, this is hard to believe," I commented. "After all, you are not even from our Earth world. And what have you got to do with Pentecost, which is a sacred day in Christianity?"

"Allow me to explain," he said as if speaking to a slow learner. "The flame of the Holy Spirit, which is the Source of All, descended on the heads of disciples to catalyze their spiritual power. And where did this fire come to rest? Their hearts. This gave them the strength to travel to many lands and to embrace and love all people. This flame of love, wisdom, and divine will was anchored in their hearts and merged into one. Let me repeat this so it's clearly understood: The three-fold flame in your heart of love, wisdom, and divine will merge into one flame. This is the process that you and all humanity must currently undergo."

"Why are you speaking about this today?" I asked.

"The Source of All permitted me to teach you whatever I wanted on any other day. However, because you've had so many experiences with fire on Pentecost, you were already open to hearing our message today. The directive was clear that today I was to speak about the merging of the three-fold flame in your heart. This flame of the Source of All comes through us dragons to catalyze spiritual transformation in human beings. In the same way, we assist with the birth of the Earth into consciousness. She is merging, merging into consciousness with the Source of All."

As my dragon brother spoke, I witnessed Gaia, the Earth, rising in frequency and saw that LOVE was her strongest quality. Although I've always thought of her as a living being, it was the first time I'd emotionally felt that Gaia had a higher version of our human chakras. Intellectually, I have spoken of her rising in frequency for many years, but I'd never felt her love accompanying this transformation process. My dragon brother had opened a gateway in my heart chakra into the heart of Gaia on this sacred day of Pentecost. I was astounded by the physical and emotional revelation that was taking place in me. I could feel the energy of love moving between Gaia and my heart and I wanted to better understand the dragon's role in this.

"What exactly are you doing to help Gaia to rise in consciousness?" I asked.

"The new frequency of Gaia," Jake replied, "is currently too high and strong for the beings living on her. Therefore, we dragons were asked, demanded, suggested, begged — there is no right word in your vocabulary — to burn off the dross of the thoughtforms that humans and animals and other beings have created on this planet. We were asked to help purge whatever has taken humanity off the direct path to the Source of All. The energy of the four-plus elements moves through us to support this transformation. This change will merge the 'I' and the 'We'. The barriers that separates each of you from others will disintegrate. It's time for this to happen."

"Okay, you've explained what you're doing for the Earth and humanity, but WHY, of all the beings in the universe, have DRAGONS been charged with this mission?"

"With our qualities of magic, wisdom, and fire of transmutation, we dragons are alchemists of the highest order. You have this talent yourself."

"How do you know this?" I asked curiously.

"How can I not?" he answered, smiling. "Even if I did not hear your thoughts as clearly as I hear my own, I could see this in your energy. You are being consumed by the fire of transmutation from the inside out and the three-fold flame is merging into one within your heart. This process has been ongoing for decades of your time and is almost complete. Anyway, that is all I wish to say."

Jake closed his eyes and withdrew his energy. It was as if he had closed a door. I decided to speak to Prajnaparamita about paths to enlightenment to discover if I could reconcile Yogananda's instructions with those of my dragon friend.

After lunch, the opportunity arose. We had retired to her living room for tea and chocolate when I posed my question.

"I'm confused about something," I began. "Yogananda and his lineage of masters teach a meditation technique whereby you focus on the third eye and see yourself going through it to enlightenment. The dragon, however, says that humanity must focus on the heart."

"Both are true," Prajnaparamita answered. "There are as many paths as people walking them. The very best path is the one that serves your awakening best. Some people are naturally devotional, some flourish in serving, some have a great capacity to discriminate and others simply surrender.

"Feminine and masculine qualities awaken in everybody," she continued. "A clear mind warms the heart and a warm heart will clarify the mind. There is no 'jnani' (follower on the path of wisdom) without an inner 'bhakta' (follower on the path of love) and in every bhakta, a jnani is waking up. Wisdom and love are One. The bhakta comes to clarity, the jnani is overwhelmed by love. The path of insight leads you to surrender, the path of surrender leads you to insight. Awakening is total."

"That is helpful," I said to her, "I've always felt that my strength was wisdom, yet, developing love is my main focus. Also, Yogananda continually states that everything we do in the day must be with devotion to the divine. This is the path of love."

Prajnaparamita, in such a clear, simple way, had put her finger on a question that had perplexed me for a long time. I felt wisdom and love merging in my heart and the process, which my dragon brother had initiated earlier, continued as my heart opened even further with her words.

It was my last day at La Roseraie de Sacha and I didn't need to teach, so I decided to return to my dragon brother to ask a few more questions. It was mid-afternoon and blazing hot by the time I arrived at my usual place. Looking for shade, I found it closer to the dragon, who appeared to be napping. As I moved my chair into place, his eyes flew open.

"Yes?" Jake asked, displaying his long, pointed teeth.

Quickly moving my chair back two paces, I settled my thoughts into what I wanted to ask.

"It occurred to me that you still haven't told me about your relationship with Mahavatar Babaji. After all, he was the one who instructed me to speak with dragons."

"Very well," he said. "I was going to speak about him when I discussed life in our dragon world; still, I could give you a taste now. Mahavatar Babaji has often been in our world and he is a saint among us. Many great beings have come to our world to work with us in the same way as dragons go to other worlds to help other races. Love and compassion — qualities that humanity values — are not our strongest gifts, or at least not in the way that you would see, feel, or know them. For that reason, Mahavatar Babaji has been in our world to help dragons know, more deeply, the strength of love and compassion."

"I find it interesting," I interjected, "that you tell me and other humans that we need to develop love in our hearts when you need to do the same thing. It seems to me that it's a strange message for you to teach when it's your weakness."

"You have only understood half of what I've advised you to develop," he answered impatiently. "All three aspects of love, wisdom, and divine will must be in balance for you to unite the three-fold flame in your heart."

Looking at me with a sly gleam in his eye, he posed the question, "Which flame do you think is the strength of dragons?"

"I'd guess will," I answered, looking at his teeth, "but you previously mentioned wisdom as one of your qualities."

"Correct," he said, "Dragon's strength is their power; what weakens us, we avoid. Every race has a gift, a strength, and a weakness. And, to answer your original question, Mahavatar Babaji helps us in two ways. Firstly, he has such a strong will that he can moderate our power for us to better work with humanity. Secondly, he has such strong love and compassion that he helps us develop compassion and service to other races."

"You say that Mahavatar Babaji goes to your dragon world. Does he manifest in a human body like he does on Earth?"

"He can choose. He can manifest either a human or a dragon body, or he can send a hologram of either form to our world in the same way that we send holograms to you. He has done both. The advantage of manifesting a body is that the physical rooting is stronger between him and us. One of his greatest services is assisting individuals and evolving races. He specializes in giving assignments to both individuals and races for what they need to develop as their next step."

Although I was fascinated by what I was hearing, due to the heat and my full stomach, I started to nod off.

"Wake up!" Jake shouted and I was fully awake immediately with my heart pounding.

"After eating a large meal, it's hard for you to maintain your attention and not fall unconscious." Deciding to pull back his volume, he continued, "It's a drain on your physical body, but it's a greater drain on your spiritual body to talk with us in such high frequencies. You are at the maximum of what you are currently capable. Take time to relax. Nurture yourself this afternoon. Recharge. You are to dedicate yourself to listening to us and writing. This is the best service you can give. Even as you were asked to present the world of the elementals to humanity, you need to present the world of the dragons. People need to be aware that dragons are already here, birthing the Earth."

"You just stated that I was at the limit of what I am spiritually capable. What if the information you wish to relate is beyond my capability?"

"There is no such thing as incompetence or inadequacy. You, like me, were prepared and chosen for this purpose," he said, exhaling deeply with exaggerated patience.

Saying goodbye to Jake, I slowly got to my feet and, putting on my sunhat and sunglasses, walked back to my room and fell into bed. Christoph and I were embarking on the eight-hour drive to Germany the next morning and I needed a good night's sleep. I looked forward to a day or two off from speaking with Jake while, at the same time, I hoped he would be in Germany to continue our conversation. So far, my dragon brother had dictated the topics he wanted me to know about, but I still had many questions to ask him.

Dragons and Holograms

Let me say a bit about Christoph. We first met 20 years ago when he attended a workshop on working with elementals that I was teaching in southern Germany. Helping the Earth was a lifetime interest of his as he trained as a biodynamic organic farmer. Since then, Christoph and his wife Katharina have studied with me and have often visited my partner, Simon, and me in Canada and we have visited them in Germany. Sadly, Katharina died a few years ago, but Christoph continues to organize my European workshops and meditation retreats and we have become good friends. He lives in the Black Forest on a large property with fruit trees, bees, and a meadow backed by a lovely forest.

The morning after our long drive from France to Germany, we were finishing breakfast when Christoph announced, "I have to go to see the bees, would you like to come?"

He gave me a beekeeper's net to place over my head while he donned the complete outfit, and we set off down the path to the hut where the beehives were. The hut was located in the shade on the outskirts of a meadow that was full of wildflowers. The location was a bee heaven. Christoph, securing the net over his head, entered the hut to see what had occurred during his three-day absence. I stayed back and waited for a signal to enter. Not a minute later, he called, "Tanis, come, look at this. It's unbelievable."

At my home in Canada, I look after wild mason bees, but I don't raise honeybees, so I wasn't certain what I was supposed to see.

Christoph picked up a flat, mesh tray covered with hundreds of bees and pointed to the honey cones in it. "The tray wasn't set up in a bee box; yet, the bees have come to it anyway," he said beaming. "I've never seen anything like this. I didn't have time to build the box and stack the trays in it before driving to France, so I left the empty tray on the shelf beside the other beehive."

We looked at each other and started to laugh. "I guess our meditation to call the bees to the hive in France called them here," I said.

"Absolutely," he agreed. "Look, here's a queen, so it will be a healthy hive. I've got to immediately put together the other hive for them."

Many months later, Christoph told me that the new hive produced twice as much honey as all his other ones. It's always good to be reminded about the power of meditation to manifest what you want.

After I left him to build the new hive, I went to look for a place that I felt my dragon friend would like. I chose a half-sunny, half-shaded, quiet spot by a small river. We would not be disturbed there and he would have space in which to land and be comfortable. Still, as I sat down, I wasn't sure if Jake would come. Listening to the soft singing of the nearby river, I closed my eyes, took a few deep breaths, and telepathically sought him. He appeared in the shade at once with his dark body blending into the background.

"Have no fear, I plan to continue our conversation," he said, as he picked up my doubts. "However, you should understand that your human time and our dragon time are not the same. When an entire day has passed for you, it's only a minute for us. You waited for one year to speak with me, but it was more like one day for me in my dragon world. We are not immortal, but we are extremely long-lived. Humans, likewise, will have very long lives when they dwell in the higher astral frequency in which we live."

"When will that be?" I asked, hoping for an answer consisting of sooner not later.

"It's not far in your future, so don't concern yourself. Wayshowers in your world already access higher astral and causal realms, and humanity, as a whole, is currently moving consciously through lower astral realms. There are many frequency levels and worlds in the astral realm. As individuals focus on positive and not negative emotions, their frequency will rise. Some individuals will begin to hear beings speaking to them from these worlds; others will see these worlds in their dreams, or have intuitive visions and glimpses."

"This is hopeful," I said, reassured that humanity was moving forward. "Nevertheless, at present, I'm personally concerned about my ability to accurately hear what you're saying. This is essential if I have the responsibility to write a book to pass on your information."

"You can only understand our world if you understand the way I'm teaching," Jake answered. "We are laying the foundation of understanding in your cells so that what we say is rooted in you. Writing a book doesn't only consist of speaking with us and then transferring the information into a book that can be read by humans. No, no, no, no. How silly."

"Then what do you want me to do?" I asked, confused. "If it's something I can do, I will, however, you have to be clear about what you want."

"Right," my dragon brother replied. "We want you to build a bridge not only with one thin thread but a wide bridge between the dragon and human worlds. We contacted you because your work has been to create pathways between worlds. You did this between the human and elemental realms. Now we want you to create a pathway so that humans can walk from the physical frequency of the Earth up through the higher astral frequencies to our world."

"And you think I'm capable of doing this?" I asked, seeking reassurance. "It's one thing to work with elementals who live in a relatively low astral frequency and quite another to work with you who live in a much higher one."

"Going to the elemental world was easy for you. Now we want you to stretch. You've done it before. You went to higher frequencies to receive the information to write *Decoding Your Destiny,* so you can do it." [3]

"It took me 12 years before I felt competent to teach what I'd learned when I wrote that book. And I was younger and fitter and …" I said.

Jake interrupted me by saying, "It took 12 years because you needed to anchor what you had learned in higher frequencies in the cells of your physical body. What humans don't fully understand is that they must fully embody new ideas, thoughts, and beliefs from higher frequencies. Humans cannot grasp what I'm saying only on a mental level. It must live, live in them, which means they have to clear away old concepts, old ideas, old roles. Letting go of cultural and family ways of viewing reality. Only then does the space open in the etheric and physical worlds where these new frequencies can root."

"For decades," I responded, "I've identified and transformed my outmoded thoughtforms and I've taught others to do the same. Is this what you're saying?"

"Exactly," Jake said. "Old thoughtforms must be eliminated and transformed to create fertile soil for new, higher ideas. We dragons say 'frequencies' and 'knowings', instead of 'ideas'. The ideational world, where dragons live, is close to the frequency where demigods and advanced human masters reside. Through thought, these beings can create form in the dragon world, as well as in the physical and astral worlds of humanity, and the somewhat higher astral world of elementals."

"Amazing that human masters can do this. Can you do it too?" I asked.

"Through balancing the elements of earth, air, fire, water, and even higher elements, I have created an advanced holographic form to reach you. Because I'm a young dragon, it takes energy to manifest my form in your lower frequency. Our older dragons can create a hologram of a world, and the beings of that world, to teach younger dragons what that world is like. You could say that this way of learning is our equivalent of books."

"Have some of the dragons which people have seen over the centuries been holograms?" I asked, wanting to make sure that I fully understood what he was saying.

"Our holograms are so advanced that they appear real to you," Jake answered. "In fact, what you think of as your physical body is also a hologram. Only the eternal part of you, the I that is We, is real.

Dragons who come to your world can be either an astral hologram, like me, or a more physical hologram, like you. They are observers — except for the throwbacks that I discussed previously — and both the observers and throwbacks have a strict message not to interfere with human evolution. Dragons may also go into the center of the Earth to be with the beings there, and they may go to other worlds, such as that of the merpeople."

"Hold on," I said, mentally flashing a red stop sign in front of his holographic eyes. "Every time you introduce a topic, such as you and I being different kinds of holograms, I want to discuss it further, but you are continually chomping at the bit to get on to another topic, such as beings in the center of the Earth and merpeople. Can't we stop and go into more depth about holograms, before gallivanting off to merpeople?"

"Hahaha!" he laughed amused. "First of all, it's not my job to discuss merpeople with you, there will be another to do this."

"Stop! Stop! What's this about someone else speaking to me about merpeople? You can't just drop that into our conversation and then move on," I said, frustrated.

"You're right. I probably shouldn't have said anything about merpeople," he said, somewhat abashed, before quickly changing the subject. "Regarding your question about how you and I are different kinds of holograms, I'll explain. Holograms are created by thought. If you are in the causal or astral realms, you create holograms through thought. You refer to them as thoughtforms. Then, if you are attracted to the physical reality, these thoughtforms eventually become physical thoughtforms that you believe are solid. You think your personality, your 'me', is real. Your belief is erroneous. It is a thoughtform, which

I call a hologram. To put it simply, I'm a higher-level thoughtform, or hologram, than you. The real you, and the real me, are the soul, which is united with the Source of All. Now, is that clear?"

"Yes, and thank you for taking the time to explain. I appreciate it when you allow me an opportunity to ask questions," I answered, giving what I hoped was encouragement for him to do this in future.

"Well and good. I think this is enough for today," Jake said, fading into the shade and disappearing.

After he had left, I remained by the river to digest what he'd said. All too often, I have the habit of racing from one thing to another without allowing sufficient time for digestion. Sitting by the river, I meditated deeply on our conversation. In doing so, I realized that the hologram that I thought of as 'me' existed not only in the physical but also in astral and causal realms. Furthermore, because one can travel by thought in these realms, these frequencies, I probably could visit many worlds. For instance, the dragon world. Although it was nice that Jake had come to my world, I was curious to visit his and I hoped he would take me to it.

As soon as I had this thought, I realized that I was removing myself from the present moment and racing to a desired future. To return to the present, I took several deep breaths, closed my eyes, and resumed meditating, knowing that all was perfect the way it was and no future was more desirable than another.

After some time, I slowly opened my eyes and walked into the warm sun. The meadow was filled with diverse wildflowers and lovely scents arose from healthy plants. Nothing could be more full of life than being exactly where I was at that moment. Opening my ears, I heard the happy gurgling of the river, the busy buzzing of the bees, and I was stroked by the soft caress of the breeze. My senses were filled with beauty and I felt immensely grateful for my life on this wonderful planet. No longer did I long to leave and go to the dragon world; instead, I was content to be exactly where I was.

Evolution of Humanity and the Earth

A day passed and no dragon. I had a hunch that he'd telepathically picked up that I needed a day off to prepare for the week-long meditation retreat that I was leading in the Black Forest. It was a lovely day and Christoph and I went for a forest walk, enjoyed a great meal, and did my laundry. These grounding activities were a great counterbalance to dragon talks. No longer was I concerned that Jake would end our conversations; therefore, I could fully appreciate time without them.

Physically and emotionally well rested, I returned the following day to my seat by the river to find out if my dragon brother would speak with me. I didn't have long to wait before he appeared.

"You live such puny lives," he began straightaway. "You don't like the word 'puny', but this is what it is to us. Our lives are very, very long. Thousands and thousands of years long in your time. You think the life of an insect or a hummingbird is short. We dragons look at you the same way that you look at such beings who aren't as evolved as you."

"I'm not pleased with your comparison, especially after having had such a great day yesterday. This is a real downer."

"Let's put it another way," he said, trying to reframe his words in a more attractive light. "I'm talking about how, compared to dragon consciousness, you seem so undeveloped at this stage of your evolution."

"Can you put this more agreeably?" I asked sarcastically. "After all, you chose me, the insect. I didn't choose to speak with you."

Noticing the humor underlying my tone, he chortled and replied, "You admire a hummingbird that can fly speedily in four directions; likewise, we admire your gifts. You have pets, such as birds, cats, and dogs, for which you feel responsible; similarly, some of our lineages feel the same about you."

"Getting a bit better. Now, humans — including me, by the way — have moved from being insects to dogs. Why do you bother with us? I'm sure you must have more interesting beings with whom to associate."

"We dragons have been with you from the beginning of your journey. When the Earth, Gaia, was forming and the call went out from the Source of All to help catalyze and birth this new planet, we came. We were excited and curious because our race is curious. And when I say excited, it's a sense of... Hmmm... Hmmm, we'll be there at the beginning. We looked forward to seeing all the species, the Earth, and the Solar System develop."

"You mention 'species'. Which species are you referring to?" I said, wanting to be sure I made no assumptions.

"Humanity, birds, animals, insects, and gems and crystals interested us although none of you were physical then. You were only etheric seeds. Also, we were interested in elementals who were to develop in an astral frequency world on your planet. We wanted to be involved in birthing you along the path the Source of All was indicating. We dragons could contribute our special gift of balancing the elements that were needed on your planet for you to evolve in the way the Source of All saw fit."

"Did all ages and lineages of dragons come?" I asked, seeking clarification.

Jake seemed not to mind my questions and answered, "Among us were older ones, mature ones, and even younger ones. Younger ones came in a student role to learn from the older ones how to help birth a planet. Our indigo lineage was specially represented," he added proudly, "as birthing planets is our gift. This was not the first time in our long history that we had been involved in birthing a planet."

"Do other races at your level of consciousness also help in the birthing of planets and solar systems?"

"Of course. It is the responsibility of any individual or race to help those less developed. You know that, so why ask?"

"I ask for confirmation. Isn't that a valid reason?" I responded, eager to hear his reply.

"When you are in higher frequencies, confirmation from others is not important because you are aligned with the Source of All," he answered kindly. "Still, responsibilities increase with consciousness, and because our old ones are balanced in the four and higher elements their participation was especially necessary. Part of the wisdom teaching of our old ones is to witness the birth and evolution of conscious races on various planets. Therefore, we return to observe and witness the evolution of humanity and Gaia. All is evolving according to the unfolding of your gifts and your divine potential. We helped to plant the seeds and to create the right environment for the seeds to grow."

I was busy considering what my dragon brother had just said when he leaped in an unexpected direction.

"We're especially interested in your crystals and gems. We have a talent for knowing the potential of each crystal, gem, and the soil from which these minerals are formed. We have a similar relationship with minerals as you have with plants and animals. You eat plants and animals for energy and, at this stage in dragon evolution, minerals and gems are our energy source. However, we know that taking energy from crystals and gems won't be necessary in our future evolution."

"If dragons have a special gift to help develop gems, were there other races who assisted with the development of humanity?" I asked, wanting to return to what was of most interest to me.

"Dragons worked with the Els from Sirius on the birthing project. The Els are creators of form and their strength is in visualization and manifestation. Their form was more aligned with the human and animal forms, whereas dragons were more aligned with the form of the Earth itself and the mineral kingdoms. That being said, the human form needs minerals for healing and energy, so the Els and dragons shared information. The dragon's emphasis was putting together all elements in the lower form world and lending the fire of transmutation to this process. The fire that we breathe forth is not one element. It works with the frequencies of the earth, air, fire, and water elements. Our fire is catalytic, transformational, and transmutational.

The elementals, angels, and other races helped to build the form; then the dragons catalyzed this form. We are messengers. We are agents. We are servants in this process. Although others helped with their particular gifts, the Els and dragons were the most needed.

Both of our races are wise, wise beyond your understanding of wise, so we have an affinity. Other races have other gifts."

"Everything you choose to speak about is interesting," I said, "but I am increasingly curious to learn more about your dragon homeworld instead of always focusing on mine."

"I understand your desire to know more about our homeworld and I'll share this with you later. However, it's not only important for you to understand our homeworld, it's also essential that you understand our relationship with humanity and Gaia. We're building a bridge, a grid of light between humans and dragons, to create a path of understanding for others to walk. This is why I weave this story together as I do."

"Okay, I get it and I'll be patient," I agreed. "One of the reasons I feel connected with what you say about dragons helping to birth the Earth is that I had a powerful vision of the great Cosmic Dragon doing that. My vision happened many decades ago, but it was probably more like a year in your dragon time. I was in a medicine ceremony and had smoked a combination of hallucinogenic plants. Not feeling well, I lay down under the stars where for hours I observed a great dragon flying through the stars. She was translucent and I could see the stars through her body. She was aware of me looking at her and she also looked at me. I knew she was birthing the Earth, Gaia, into becoming a conscious planet."

"You call her the Cosmic Dragon. What you saw were highly evolved ancient dragons of many lineages. These dragons are our equivalent of highly evolved enlightened masters. They work collaboratively in all frequencies to embrace Gaia and catalyze her to her next stage in evolution."

"I saw one dragon, not many, why is that?"

"They merged their frequencies into one and you saw the result of the merged being. Your vision is correct, so don't doubt yourself. But because this happens at very high frequencies, your interpretation is not entirely accurate."

"It's great that my vision is correct; yet, it's not great that my interpretation is inaccurate," I replied, thinking of my responsibility to translate what he was saying without error.

"Your vision is many decades old and you're able to access much higher frequencies now," Jake said, reassuring me. "You and humanity are in the nesting stage. Although you are still in the nest, you have cracks in the energetic shell that surrounds your physical, astral, and causal bodies. Both humanity's and your planet's shells are cracking to allow in higher frequencies from the Source of All and other conscious worlds. Both humans and Gaia are starting to hatch, to be reborn into consciousness."

"How exactly do you crack us?" I asked, imagining him clutching me in his talons.

"You crack yourself from inside at the same time as we dragons crack you from outside. It's the appropriate timing from the Source of All. It's not that we force anything on you. It's more that we hatch you. We embrace you. The Cosmic Dragon oversees this process for Gaia. Many conscious beings at many levels of knowing, such as the Els, angels, and dragons, are involved in this process. We dragons descend to the lowest frequencies where we can be effective to assist with birthing humans into higher frequencies."

"Could you be more specific?" I inquired.

"Certainly," Jake replied. "The Earth, Gaia, wishes to return to the Source of All. She is throwing off all that is of a lower frequency.

This consists of the old structures that humans have built and their old thoughtforms."

"I can understand the destruction of old organizational structures; however, does the Earth care about killing humans and animals?" I asked, thinking of the deaths of so many.

"Gaia notes the loss of each of its cells, which could be an animal, or an insect, or a flower, or a human being. These are all cells in her body. She created them. She is aligning herself to what is needed to move to a higher frequency. Gaia is helping to crack her own shell. This is why volcanoes, earthquakes, and hurricanes are increasing. She is widening the gaps between the tectonic plates on which the land masses dwell in order to move to a higher frequency. Gaia is moving in obedience to the Divine plan and, in doing so, she is assisting human beings to do the same. Each being on Earth is being assisted both by Gaia and by Spirit to move to a higher frequency although it may not look this way to your limited perspective."

He must have sensed me resisting what he was saying for he decided on a different, more sensitive, approach.

"You feel that I distance myself from you. You feel my neutral emotions and interpret them as a lack of love. This is your interpretation of the frequency of knowing from which I am speaking. This frequency is higher than the frequency of emotion. It's the frequency in which being and doing are balanced. There are neither preferences nor desires — in the way that one conceives of desires — when one is merged with the Source of All. Personal desires are burned away and all that remains is what you call the authentic Self. This vessel is filled to overflowing by the Source of All and one is a willing, conscious co-creator with the Source of All. This is your next stage in evolution.

"This is what we dragons know, what we teach. Hmmm ... Hmmm ... Teach is a limited word, it's more like we *are* it. Whether we use words that you translate through clairvoyance, clairaudience, and clairsentience, what is occurring is not so much a teaching as infiltrating, impregnating, catalyzing, transforming, transmuting. These words are more appropriate for the process in which you and I are engaged."

I was on the point of interrupting when he gave me a 'no ... wait!' look. I resumed listening and hoped I would remember what I was going to ask.

"At this point in humanity's evolution, our fire is needed to burn away your old self-limiting thoughtforms. We dissolve old illusions, beliefs, and habits on which your previous evolution is based. Gaia cooperates with this process. Simultaneously, both your Sun and Earth are raising their frequency from within. This process shifts your planet's tectonic plates that trigger volcanoes and weather patterns, which, in turn, release stuck areas and free energies that have been imposed on it by humanity and by the Source of All during your former stage of evolution."

He focused his piercing golden eyes on me and waited for me to ask one of the many questions that had arisen during his explanation.

"I find it interesting that it's not just humanity, but the Source of All that has supported old thoughtforms on our Earth. Why is that?"

"Animals and even plants have thoughtforms," my dragon brother replied, keen to exhibit his advanced knowledge. "These thoughtforms are more akin to the old habits of their species. During the rise in frequency caused by the Source of All, the Sun, and the Earth, the old thoughtforms of limitation for their species are released so they also can merge into the knowing of which we speak. This process affects gems, minerals, soil, insects, worms… basically everything."

"Because I was more concerned with humanity, I haven't seriously considered that the frequency of all Earth beings would rise."

"This is natural," he acknowledged. "Humans have viewed all species through their human lens and concentrated on their own evolution until now, but this will change. In higher frequencies, you and others are already aligned to the Source of All. You only need to awaken to know this."

I felt full of information and each conversation with my dragon brother raised more questions than answers.

"This is enough for today," he said, noticing my fatigue. "For the next few weeks, enjoy the people in the workshops. Teaching will help and not detract from the energy you need to continue our work together. Your frequency rises when you are engaged in spiritual teaching. Yes, you may be physically tired, but you are spiritually energized and your heart opens more fully through assisting others. Enjoy your time digesting what you and I have spoken of, and I will soon begin speaking of our homeworld."

"When do you want to speak with me again?" I asked, wanting clarification before he left for an undisclosed time.

"The timing isn't as important as the accuracy of what I would like to tell you," Jake answered. "So far, I've been focusing on the relationship between dragons and humans. When we can continue without interruption, I wish to focus on our dragon world. However, it's not the right time yet. For this, you will need to have quiet because our world is at a much higher frequency than what you normally experience. Your understanding and comprehension are limited because our way of thinking and being is different from yours."

"More hurdles," I said. "Are you saying that it's easier for me to understand when you come to my world as a hologram than it will be for me to go to your world?"

"I'll give you a personal example," he replied. "When you teach, you enter the thoughtforms and frequencies of the country. Think back some 25 years and remember the headaches you experienced with the mental thoughtforms when you first taught in Germany. It took you a few trips to Germany before your body could freely enter German thoughtforms. Likewise, it will be a physical and spiritual effort for you to be in our dragon world and it will be taxing on your body. Yet, this is necessary."

"Isn't there an easier way?" I asked, remembering the pain of my first years of teaching in Germany.

"You're not a passive channel," Jake replied. "You're a co-creator in our journey together and we must meet in my world not only in yours. It's not only difficult for you to come to my world, it's also difficult for me to come to yours because of the lower frequency. For me, it feels like being trapped in thick mud. There are no errors. What you're doing thus far is accurate and true. We are satisfied. Hmmm...Hmmm... When you and I have established a relationship in my homeworld, like we've been doing in yours, you can speak with our brood mother. Our mother dragon. And hopefully after that, you can speak with our old sire."

"Thanks for explaining your situation as I didn't fully understand. Because you and the other dragons feel I can travel to your world, I have faith that I can. I look forward to speaking with you again after I'm home in Canada. Until then, rest and be well."

Following my dragon brother's departure, I sat by the river for a long time soaking in the peace there. I was awed by the privilege of being chosen to speak with the dragons and my insecurities were evaporating. Slowly, yes, but they were leaving. It was amazing the breadth and depth of his knowledge of humanity and Gaia's evolution, and I was grateful more than ever that it was my young dragon brother, not an older dragon, who had been chosen to speak with me. I could not imagine how I would have dealt with an older one, but, as he said, I was soon to find out.

Encounter with the Ruby Dragon

Two months came and went before I was ready to communicate with Jake. During that time, I returned home to Canada and transcribed what he'd told me into written form. It was summer and summer is playtime, especially when I'd been working away. Therefore, I availed myself of the warm weather to swim in the ocean and sleep nightly under the stars. Indulging myself and breaking old responsible, time-constraining patterns felt good and much needed. In part, I knew that I was readying myself for the next installment of *The Dragon's Tale* but there was no rush. Then one day, with fall coming, I heard a powerful, ancient dragon voice command me, "You must come to Iceland now!"

This was not the first time I'd been called to go to Iceland. I had tried and been unsuccessful on two separate occasions. The last time was several years ago when I organized an Icelandic tour and 30 individuals from around the world registered to join me. Unfortunately, the pandemic hit and the tour was canceled. This time, I knew from the voice that I MUST go and I booked a flight. My friend Christoph had been registered for the canceled tour and he asked to join me.

He offered to drive and I was relieved so that I could concentrate on communicating with dragons, and who knows, maybe some elementals.

It's well known that most Icelanders believe in elementals, which they refer to as the 'huldufólk' or 'hidden people', but I'd never heard of them believing in dragons. Why, then, must I go? This question was uppermost on my mind as the plane landed and, checking in the guidebook, I hightailed it to Reykjavik's largest bookstore where I hoped to find leads to locations where dragons had been spotted.

Approaching a young man who worked there, I asked, "Do you have any books on dragons in Iceland?"

He looked confused, so I rephrased my question, "Are there myths about dragons in Iceland?"

I could see the wheels turning as he considered my request, but his answer was not the one I sought. "Most of our stories are about trolls, the huldufólk, and ghosts," he replied, leading me to the section where there were books on those topics. I perused the shelves without success on the topic of dragons and left the store disappointed. There was no point worrying about what was not happening. Iceland is a physically beautiful country, so I might as well play tourist and enjoy myself.

The following day, after consulting our maps, Christoph and I set off driving along the south coast where we visited cascading waterfalls, turquoise glaciers, and ever-changing vistas. I was having such a good time touring that I was almost disappointed when three days later, near Skogar, I heard a dragon telepathically say, "Stop beside that glacier on the left."

Christoph stopped the car where the dragon indicated and we got out. The wind was brutal, gale-force, and howling. I tried to walk to the glacier, but I literally couldn't move forward. Fortunately, Christoph is a stocky guy and he was able to physically anchor me to the ground as I struggled to where the dragon wanted me. Christoph put me behind a small boulder that offered some protection and withdrew to guard my privacy. Crouched behind the boulder with the wind wailing around me, I hunkered down to wait. I wasn't pleased with the dragon's timing and my hands were frozen by the time I saw a dragon approaching.

Buffeted by the wind, the scales on his back were raised and the crest on his head was blown back. Squinting his eyes to keep out the wind, he happily tossed his head, showing that he, unlike me, loved the wild weather. The dragon was smaller and younger than I had anticipated given the strength of the sending that I had originally received to come to Iceland. He was an indigo color like Jake, which made me wonder if they knew each other.

"I'm not the one who c...c...called you," the young dragon said in way of a greeting. "Jaakelousekindvron (huff... grunt... groan) told me you'd be in Iceland, so I decided to meet you. Later, you'll meet the old dragon, the wise protector, who sent you the message."

The young male dragon hesitated and stuttered as he spoke and I realized he was lonely — a word I wouldn't usually associate with a dragon. I attempted to keep my perceptions of his loneliness private for I didn't wish to insult him. Dragons can be prickly. Not having spoken with a human before and not picking up my thoughts, he launched into an explanation of what he was doing in Iceland.

"We dragons have been involved in helping to form Iceland," he said, choosing the topic he wished to discuss.

He might enjoy speaking with a human, I thought, so I might as well get him used to my questions right from the beginning.

"How are you doing that?" I asked, attempting to engage him in a discussion.

"We are involved in helping to create volcanoes t... t... to help the Earth, Gaia, let off steam."

I never knew that dragons might stutter and I wondered if his stuttering had anything to do with why a relatively young dragon would be in Iceland instead of in his world. I clamped down hard on my outgoing thoughts and was successful in keeping this idea private too.

"We dragons are making a b... b... bridge between the newest earth that wants to be born here and the older earth on the other continents. The rainbows you see daily in Iceland are making a rainbow bridge to the new Earth."

"How exactly are dragons building the bridge?" I asked, wanting him to be more specific.

"Isn't it obvious?" he answered. As he spoke, he shuffled from foot to foot in nervousness and I could tell he was struggling with how to effectively communicate with a human. I could only guess that he hadn't had Jake's training that qualified him to speak with humans and wondered if this fledgling had taken it upon himself to speak to me. Well, dragons are curious and that could explain it, I thought to myself.

Making a decision, the young indigo dragon continued, "Dragons can work with all elements: earth, air, fire, water. Here there is very rough wind th... th... that we are experiencing right now. That's the air. Also, Iceland has rough freezing seas near the Arctic Circle with dramatic waterfalls tumbling off the glaciers. That's the water. At the same time, there are active volcanoes spewing fire that emerges from the earth. Iceland is a land of extremes and people live here with extreme elements. This is what the new Earth will be like."

"Okay," I granted, "but I'm still unclear about what this has to do with you and perhaps other dragons?" I wasn't trying to increase his insecurities, but I did want to understand his message."

"Dragons are helping the Earth, Gaia, to rebirth itself," he replied, sounding a bit disconcerted by my lack of understanding. "We work in Iceland with the volcanoes and the shifting of the tectonic plates. For us, the shifting of the plates is like cracking the egg of a little chicken so it can hatch. We help to hatch Gaia. The Eurasian plate meets the North American plate in Iceland and this place is a crossroads within the Earth. This land is a sacred land f...f...for dragons. In many ways, the dragon world of higher frequencies is a tamed environment for us. In Iceland, we like the drama, th...th...the newness, the spontaneity, the uncensored. This is all I wanted to say to you."

"Thanks for your explanation," I said, "I appreciate it." I tried to reassure him that he'd done a good job as I certainly didn't want to worsen his lack of confidence.

The young male didn't leave; instead, he huffed and cleared his throat and looked uncertain as to how to proceed. Finally, he asked, "Actually, I have a request."

"Of course, what is it?"

My effort to assure him appeared to work as he nodded and said, "C...c...could you give me a nickname like Jake?"

Who would have thought that human nicknames would be so popular with dragons? Tuning into his vibration, I listened for what word fit his shy, self-effacing presence.

"Harold," I said. "Your nickname is Harold."

"I love it. Harold. I'll tell Jake," he replied grinning, and disappeared.

I was tickled to have found something that humans could do to please dragons but, so far, I'd only spoken with young dragons. I didn't think the powerful old dragon who had called me to Iceland would be happy to receive a nickname. A few days later I found out, but first I met Sebastian.

Sebastian was a cultural anthropologist working in a visitor center near where I met the young indigo dragon. When I asked him if he knew any old tales of dragons in Iceland, he smiled, reached into his pocket, and pulled out an Icelandic coin to show me.

"Since the days of the Vikings, Iceland has had four protective spirits. Look here!" he said, pointing to the crest on the coin, "The dragon is the protector of the east and it's on our coin."

Taking the coin from his hand, I looked closely. Sure enough, a dragon was on the Icelandic crest. Leaving Sebastian, Christoph and I continued on our journey, and a thought niggled at me. 'Would the dragon, who had called me, be the same ancient dragon who appeared on the Icelandic coin?' Two days later, in the eastern part of Iceland, my question was answered.

Christoph and I were negotiating a mountain pass on a dirt road when I heard a booming voice. From the strength of the call, I knew it could be none other than a very powerful dragon and probably the one who had commanded me to come to Iceland. Christoph pulled over the car and ground to an immediate halt by the side of the road. Grateful that it wasn't raining and that there was no wind, I got out and started climbing towards the mound from where the call had emerged. A massive ruby-red dragon watched me approach. From its size alone, I knew this dragon was much, much older than my fledgling brother. Although outwardly androgynous, I felt that her essence was more female. She impatiently flicked her tail back and forth and her overall bearing didn't make me eager to come within her reach.

As I edged closer, she said by way of introduction, "Must you be so slow? I have much to say."

Her cool reception indicated that she'd be unwilling to speak with me for very long, so I got straight to my most important question, "Are you one of the four protectors of Iceland?"

"It's not for you to ask questions, it's for me to tell," she answered, tapping her talons in annoyance. "I have been on this island for almost a thousand of your years. Before that, I dwelled in Britain and Scandinavia because it used to be much cooler here. I prefer to dwell in remote spaces where there are no humans, and when humans first came to this place, I chased them away."

One of my inner questions must have bubbled to the surface of my thoughts because she was quick to answer.

"Yes, I had to share this place with other beings that were already here. They are what you call giants. They are not the same human lineage as you. I encountered giants before in the Glens of Antrim in Northern Ireland and in Norway where, by the way, other dragons live. The little people were also here, the trolls, and even smaller ones. The hidden people, the gnomes you say, are quite friendly to humans, but not the trolls. They and the giants prefer more remote valleys deeper in the mountains. They were here before the humans came."

The power emanating from her was immense, and, from her tone, I sensed her distaste for humans. She was not friendly like Jake and Harold, and I felt dwarfed and fearful in her presence.

"Humans for me are like rats to you," she said, picking up my thoughts. "Yes, of course, I read your mind. Dragons grow in power as they age and our ruby lineage has especially strong energy. I know you're writing a book with an indigo fledgling. I'm the first old one that you've met. What I've seen and know are very different from anything a fledgling could tell you."

Her simple words were layered with stacks of meaning. She was ancient compared with my dragon brother and she thought that I should feel honored by her willingness to speak with me. At the same time, she knew it was her duty, her responsibility to communicate with this insignificant human…even though she didn't want to be bothered. Hence her impatience, from which she made no effort to spare me.

"Why did I come to Earth, you ask? I've been here many thousands of years. I came to your world when there were many earthquakes, volcanoes, and earth changes, before the time you refer to as Atlantis."

She continued to anticipate my thoughts even before I did, and it was unnerving being so open in her powerful frosty presence.

"And yes, I am the same dragon that is the Red Dragon of Wales. I was in Wales before I came to Iceland and all of Wales was my territory. Even now I can go to the mountains of Wales if I wish. I like mountains, but I prefer the heat of the volcanos in Iceland. Here, I can bathe in hot pools and rest in lava beds where hot stones are thrown up from the interior of the earth. This is very desirable."

As she spoke, I reflected on how it would feel to be thousands of years old and alone and she must have picked up my feeling of sympathy.

"Do I feel lonely? Not at all," she said proudly, quickly correcting my human assumption. "I have no desire to be with others of my kind. I am not a throwback. I am a pioneer. I have chosen to be here.

I know that your fledgling brother did not tell you that other dragons, other than throwbacks and their caretakers, dwelled on Gaia, but they do. This whole area is my area. I won't say I look after it. I would say more...Hmmm...Hmmm... something like enjoy it, something like protect it. Hmmm... something like help evolve it because I like to help Gaia to evolve. I am less concerned with helping humans. As Gaia moves into her next cycle, there will be more earthquakes, more volcanoes, and this will be a good time for me to be here. I physically enjoy Iceland, and I can help to build a bridge from Gaia's lower frequency to the higher frequency she will move into."

Because the ruby dragon had lived for so long in the Earth's lower frequency, I wondered if she was stuck here like the throwbacks and sympathy started to seep through my thoughts again.

She threw off my concern by asserting, "By exerting a great deal of energy, I could return to the dragon world even now should I want, but, as you surmised, it would not be easy. Because I have been in Gaia's lower frequencies for so long, my body has become accustomed to them."

I sensed that our conversation was ending, so I decided to ask a specific question, "Do you have a message for humans that you would like me to put in the book?"

"I have no particular message for humans. You can share what I've said. I chose for you to see me and others with spiritual vision can also see me. However, I am tired of being near the road with the traffic. Now, I am going deeper into the interior where I can be alone again to soak up energy and to help raise the frequency of Gaia. The Earth, Gaia, is my task. Not humans, not elementals, not giants. Anyway, I've said what I wanted to say."

The ancient ruby dragon rose into the air and headed for the high mountains further inland. I reflected on what she'd said. I didn't know why she had called me to Iceland as she was not interested in humans. Ahhh, of course. She wished me to experience the Icelandic energy. It, like her, was a powerful transformative force and, somehow, I understood that her red color had to do with raw energy and that her energy was needed in the transformation process of the Earth. It wasn't just her strength that came with age, but her color was significant.

Later when I visited the dragon world, I learned more about the importance of her ruby-red color. However, at that moment, I understood that she and Iceland were both involved in catalyzing my energy to make me a better vessel to write about the birth of the New Earth and THAT was important to her. I felt the time approaching when I would be able to visit the dragon world to learn more about their evolution, environment, and lineages.

The Dragon World

Two Dragon Evolutions

I dream. I find myself in a large cave with a small woman. I follow her as she walks into narrower and narrower sections of the cave until she finally crawls through a body-hugging tunnel. I lower myself onto my belly and start crawling through the tunnel only to get stuck midway. My friend has gone on. I am alone. I try to go forward and cannot. I try to back up and cannot. I'm firmly stuck. Fearful thoughts occur. What if rats come down the tunnel and eat my face and body while I'm still alive? What if my lungs collapse and I cannot breathe? Then a positive thought arises. What if I relax and surrender? If I do this, I feel that the tunnel will expand and I'll be able to crawl through to the other side, the side from which light emerges. I awaken knowing this is the solution and what Spirit calls for.

Lying in bed, I rehashed the dream. The cave was reminiscent of the dragon's cave in which I'd found myself many decades ago. Furthermore, my dragon brother had been encouraging me to lighten my frequency, so I could visit his homeworld. I sensed that the smaller, lighter woman whom I'd followed had abided with his recommendation and that, by surrendering to the process, I would be able to go to the dragon world. Such a powerful dream indicated that it was time to speak with Jake again. Several months had elapsed since our last conversation in Germany, and now that I was back home in Canada, I needed to find the ideal place he'd like for our talk.

After dressing, I walked around my property to discover where he'd be comfortable. I sat on a loveseat embraced by a honeysuckle cascading down from the arbor. I looked out over the ocean and was about to contact Jake when the child next door began to wail…and didn't stop. Getting up, I walked to the other side of the property only to find the neighbors discussing plans for the day. Moving, I sought out the shade of my meditation garden and, once again, sat down.

"Close your eyes, breathe deeply, and center yourself," I heard Jake say inside my mind.

Doing as instructed, inner peace became my ally and I glimpsed him patiently awaiting me.

Finally, he cleared his throat and said, "Although it has been two months in your time, it's only been a few days in mine since we last met. There is no rush. All proceeds according to plan. It's not easy for you to hear us with your computer, your life, and travel distracting you. Speaking of traveling, you met my indigo friend in Iceland."

I opened my mouth to talk about Harold, but typical of Jake, and not waiting for my response, he launched into a topic for which I was unprepared.

"We dragons are travelers too. We love to travel not only in our world, but to all worlds. This is why we learned to fly. We weren't always flyers, you know?

"Oh, I see. You didn't know. Here, I'll show you," he sent me a clear, holographic image of the original dragons and I found myself teleported and immersed in that time.

"Yes. Yes. Originally, we were creatures of the sea," he continued with enthusiasm, as if my joining him in that early world was the most natural occurrence. "As you see, we used what are now our wings as a kind of flipper with which to steer. This is why we are so comfortable in the water and why many of your human myths speak about us being in the water. Our dragon world has beautiful, wonderful scenes in the ocean and we explored its depths. Even now we love to bathe in the shallows and soak up the sun. This is a favorite pastime of ours."

I was dragged at lightning speed from one scene to another as he spoke. I was his eyes, seeing what he saw and knowing what he knew. Just getting used to his watery existence, I was yanked forward by his next words.

"Yet, after we had explored the great depths of the sea, we became bored and decided to poke our heads into the air. Doing this, we learned how to breathe both in the water and the air. This was our first stage in conscious evolution to be able to breathe in both places. Even after it became impossible to breathe in the water, we could hold our breath for long periods by going into a semi-dormant state. In this way, we could journey in the ocean depths for hours. There are underwater caves where we could rest and we found the darkness very appealing."

Following his evolutionary journey, I experienced breathing both underwater and in the air and was flung into an earlier human life when, as a merperson, I could do the same. Jake gave me no time to enjoy my own experience and snatched me back to study me.

"What I'm sharing is part of our dragon mythology," he said, staring at me with his penetrating, golden eyes. "This is the way we learn and share information. It's quicker and more efficient and, in all ways, superior to your human books, which contain varying accounts by different authors about human stages of evolution. We dragons immediately know exactly how we evolved by being there because, in our high frequency, we can travel backward in space and time by only using thought."

His explanation allowed me to stabilize and accommodate myself to his teaching method. Knowing he intended to continue this way of instructing me, I slowed him down to ask a question.

"I'm interested to hear more about your first stage in evolution. For example, what did you eat?" I asked.

"At that time, we lived on the creatures of the sea, much as you live on animals and plants. This was our animal stage in evolution, but our curiosity brought us to the surface of the oceans. We saw land and were curious about it. Dragons have always had strong minds and we made our bodies grow legs to be able to walk on land. This was our next stage in evolution to create legs by thought."

Through his words and images, I was catapulted back in time again and saw dragons crawling onto land and, second by second, growing stronger legs until they could stand. I became dizzy moving at such accelerated speed through dragon evolution, and, hoping to slow the process, I asked a question.

"Human myths state that Asian dragons had two front and two back legs," I ventured, "whereas sometimes the dragons in Western Europe only had two back legs. Why is that?"

"I hoped to speak of this at a later time; yet, you have the habit of anticipating me," Jake said, pulling himself up to his full height. "There are two kinds of dragons because we evolved in different directions. This split is similar to when your dolphins and whales decided to leave land-based existence to become people of the sea. Our two dragon nations separated, and we ultimately moved to different frequencies. We four-legged dragons dwell in a higher astral frequency than dragons with smaller front legs, who are in a middle astral frequency. We higher-frequency dragons would state that we are the more evolved of the two; still, the ones in the lower frequency have gifts that we have lost."

As he spoke, I was pulled up and down between two worlds. When he said that the four-legged dragons were in a higher frequency, I saw him and the world I was coming to know. When he mentioned the lower-frequency dragon world, it was as if I was on a roller coaster at the top of a hill being thrust downhill at full speed. My stomach lurched. Trying to steady myself, I saw a world reminiscent of dinosaurs with lots of tall tree-like ferns. I was hesitant to set down in the strange, new environment. It oozed danger.

"They are physically larger and we are more fragile than them," said my friend, reinforcing my concerns. "Sometimes, not often, we travel to each other's worlds and ambassadors move between these two worlds to find out what would be of use to the other. For example, we higher-frequency dragons frequently obtain raw minerals and crystals from them that we need to renew our energy sources, and they receive back these charged, energized crystals from us. They use these energy sources to feed and warm themselves and to progress along their evolutionary path."

Images of large, heavily muscled dragons digging up crystals and minerals with smaller front legs sprang to mind to be replaced by smaller, leaner, and altogether more delicate dragons like Jake. Viewing these contrasting images made me happy I was dealing with the later version.

"Do the two kinds of dragons ever mate?" I asked, wondering how this would happen, and eager to hear about mating rituals.

"Very, very occasionally there can be a mating between the two, but it can be difficult since they outweigh us at least two to one. Because of the size and weight difference, it would be more likely for a male in our higher frequency to fertilize a female in the lower frequency. If there is affection between the two dragons, they can mate and create a fertile offspring. The offspring would be a hybrid of the two nations and it would be raised wherever the sire and dam decided would be best for that hatchling. The hybrid dragon would have gifts from our lineage and be able to teach and help with the evolution of those in the lower frequency."

I witnessed what he was saying through the holographic image. The male was definitely the lightweight and mating occurred because the female positioned herself in a willing, receptive position with her tail in the air. It surprised me that mating took place on land, not in the air, and I sent a telepathic message to Jake inquiring why this was.

"Because of the difference in size," he answered, "it's easier to mate on land. The sire is acting as a sperm donor in this case to help the dam produce an egg with high intelligence. They are not urged by hormones, but by a desire to raise the frequency of the lower-frequency dragons."

Anticipating my next question, my dragon brother said, "A sire from the lower-frequency dragon world will occasionally fertilize a dam in our world to produce a hybrid that is brooded and raised here. These hybrids are not treated like the unstable or emotionally challenged throwbacks we have sent to Earth and other planets. They are nurtured here to the limit of what they are capable. Then they return to the lower-frequency world to help dragons there. That hybrid is what you refer to as a bodhisattva — a being whose main purpose is to assist others to raise their consciousness."

"Do you think dragons in your higher-frequency world will ever unite with those of the lower frequency?" I inquired.

"We are their kin," Jake replied. "We are both dragons. They are physically stronger than us, and we are mentally superior to them. Because we are more advanced mentally, and value this quality above others, we sometimes can be cool. The dragons in the lower astral frequency are often more compassionate than us. They have worked longer and more diligently to develop their emotions. They had to do this, or they could have destroyed their world and other worlds because of their ferociousness. By the way, it's throwbacks from the lower-frequency dragon world who settled in Western Europe and who ate humans and destroyed towns."

His words catapulted me into our human past where I observed a town being burned by a low-flying dragon spitting fire from its mouth. The dragon's wild yellow eyes shone with hatred and he sought to destroy as many humans as he could. Archers shot arrows that easily glanced off his scales, and, extending his talons, the angry dragon clutched an archer and crushed him. Pulling out of this violent scene, I saw Jake assessing my reaction.

"Don't forget, this dragon is a throwback who has been hunted in your world," he said, offering an alternative opinion to my horror and disgust. "In their lower-frequency dragon world, they can be doting family members. Our high-frequency dams and sires, in contrast, usually don't feel a responsibility to nurture the offspring once they fledge. I don't think you'd approve of that behavior either.

The dragons in the lower frequency have more family groupings, and sires are encouraged by the dams to take a more active, friendly role with their offspring and with all hatchlings. To do this, the sires often engage in more sports and play with the young ones. So the sires, dams, and hatchlings are not as alone as we tend to be in our higher-frequency world."

"Excuse me for asking my question again, but you haven't answered," I said. "Do you think the two dragon nations might evolve together in the future?"

"It's not impossible," he said. "We have continued to interbreed for both of our purposes over thousands and thousands of years. Hmmm…, so it's possible. Dragons of both nations are beings of four elements. Both can breathe fire, fly, walk on the earth, and swim in water."

"When did the fire breathing start?" I interrupted, not wanting him to jump ahead. "You haven't explained that yet."

"I was getting to that," he said smiling at my efforts to keep him on topic. "Fire breathing started when we became land-based creatures. We couldn't run as quickly on our legs as other land-based beings, which had a head start evolving on land, but we discovered that we could use fire to attack and kill our prey. We were still carnivorous at that time."

I found myself pulled back in time witnessing the dragon's first forays into flight. As their tiny wings started to grow, they hopped along the ground spitting little gobs of fire after fleeing prey. Not being very effective, they learned as their wings grew that gliding from a cliff to catch birds in the air, or landing on top of prey from above was more successful. They eventually became lighter and ate less flesh as more weight inhibited their flight. This image evaporated and I found myself back with Jake.

"What did you eat for energy?" I asked, wondering if dragons had gone from being carnivores to vegetarians.

"We were never really drawn to the plant world," he said, poking me good-naturedly. "I should think you would realize where we get our energy based on everything we've discussed thus far."

"I'd guess gems and crystals, but I'd like to know if there was an intermediate step between eating animals for food and absorbing energy from minerals?"

"It's good to make sure of your understanding," Jake replied. "Dragons evolved from being carnivorous to absorbing energy from gems and minerals. This was the same for both the higher and lower-frequency dragons. Hmmm…Hmmm… But the dragons in the lower frequency consumed animals longer than we did. This concludes your introduction to the dragon world and our evolution."

"Before we stop, I have a few more questions. I wonder if you are still evolving and, if so, in what way?" I asked.

He exhaled with exaggerated patience indicating that he thought my question self-explanatory. Then, behaving like an indulgent lower-frequency dragon who nurtures the young ones, my dragon brother said, "Of course, we're still evolving. As we move into higher frequencies, we become less solid. We become causal beings. Thought beings. And having a physical body becomes less and less important for us. We live by uniting with the Source of All, as I've said, and the Source of All is our energy source. The dragons in the lower frequency, on the other hand, are still learning how to use minerals for energy. In fact, when we were deciding who would write about the dragon world, it was difficult to determine if it was better to ask a dragon in the lower frequency world to speak with you."

"Why was that?" I asked. I was disappointed that I'd almost been rejected by the higher-frequency dragons. Simultaneously, I was relieved that I hadn't ended up with larger, more ferocious ones.

"Choosing who should speak with you was difficult because it would be easier for you to access the middle astral frequency in which the lower-frequency dragons dwell as their world is closer to that of your Earth than our higher astral world."

"What made you decide to have a higher-frequency dragon speak with me?" I asked.

"The fact that you were brooded by our mother and that I am your nest sibling was the deciding point that led us to believe we would be able to bring you to our higher frequency to teach you about our dragon world. Also, the lower-frequency dragons have less interest in speaking with humans than we do."

"Because?" I inquired.

"They have a more difficult past with humans since you and they hunted each other. They might feel more antagonistic towards you and you towards them. Therefore, although they are more emotionally based like humans, it would not be a very beneficial meeting for either of you. That is enough for today."

After he left, I realized I was of two minds. One part of me contemplated my good fortune that he and his mother had welcomed me into their world. At the same time, I began to wonder if it would be beneficial to speak with dragons who lived in the lower astral frequency. The more I considered this possibility, the more important this idea became in my mind. It wouldn't let me go. After all, didn't those dragons deserve to be represented in *The Dragon's Tale*? I still hoped that our brood mother and sire would speak with me, but now I included the lower-frequency dragons in the list of conversations I wanted to have.

The Crystal Cave

I took my time going to my meditation garden the next day. I was relaxed because I felt that I had a foothold in the dragon world at last. Sitting in meditation, I centered myself and waited for Jake to arrive. He did not appear. Seeking him with my inner eye, I found him resting in a cave in his world. Clearly, I was to go to him. Focusing my attention on him and the cave, I landed on the ground in front of him.

"Our link is now strong enough that you can come to my world," he said, welcoming me. "It's time that you extended yourself to do this as you were becoming lazy waiting for me to come to you. Moreover, it was becoming tiresome for me."

"What? I thought you came to my garden yesterday," I said, puzzled.

"Did you see me there?" he asked, raising his eyebrow.

Thinking back, I realized that I had not seen him in a specific location. I recalled empty space surrounding him and had assumed he was in my garden. Reading my mind, he followed my thoughts.

"In reality, we met in between your world and mine," he said. "This is why you saw only black space. We thought images, holograms, can exist in space as easily as in your garden or my cave. Your frequency is now high enough that you can come to my world in thought; still, I knew you needed a transition step before doing so. For that reason, we met in deep space yesterday in the high astral, low causal frequency."

Many questions related to his surprising new information crossed my mind, and I grabbed an important one to ask.

"How can frequencies be both high astral and low causal at the same time?"

"All emotions are in the astral frequency and when your thoughts are neutral of emotion they are in the causal realm. Our dragon world — I refer to the world of our high-frequency dragons — exists in that high astral, low causal frequency range. The lower-frequency dragon world is located in a middle, astral frequency."

"And what about the Earth?" I asked, wondering about humans.

"The frequency of your planet and humans is not identical," he replied, reading my mind. "The Earth, Gaia, has been in a lower astral frequency, but she is moving now to a more middle range. You humans, on the other hand, exist in a whole gamut of frequencies depending on the day, your environment, your friends, and your thoughts. It's more accurate to ascertain your resting frequency, but there is an entire range of frequencies even then. A great many humans exist in the lowest astral realm, the majority are somewhat higher, and a few are in high astral frequencies where positive emotions of compassion, forgiveness, and love exist."

"Don't dragons vary in frequencies?" I inquired.

"Not at all. There are only slight differences in resting frequencies among us higher-frequency dragons, and these are mostly due to the dragon's age rather than his, or her, soul development."

"I think elementals vary in frequencies like humans which is according to their spiritual development," I said, thinking of all the elementals I'd known. "Why is it different for dragons?"

"Simply, the higher the frequency the more stable it is. Dragons dwell in a high frequency and humans do not. In fact, you are at the limit of what frequency you can consistently access when you come to my world. I stress the word 'consistently' because we dragons find it very difficult being with you, or any being for that matter, when your frequency wobbles between your emotional ups and downs."

"Oops," I replied with a smile, attempting to keep my frequency positive and stable.

"Hahaha. I love your humor, Tanis," he chuckled. "Humor is not one of our strong points and many young ones, such as me, appreciate it. One of the reasons I was chosen to speak with you was because, being a fledgling, I was more flexible, and capable of greater emotional frequencies, and could be more comfortable with you. But a word of advice. You are now in my world and I want to take you around to see it; therefore, you need to maintain a calm equilibrium to not upset other dragons.

"Super," I answered, excited at the prospect of seeing the dragon world for myself.

Jake re-assessed me. "Let's pause a moment. I want to prepare you for an excursion in our world."

"Whatever you recommend to make it easier is fine by me," I replied, quite willing to fall into line.

"In that case, make yourself comfortable," he said, visualizing a chair for me to sit on. "Sit in the chair, take a deep breath, relax, and become deeply receptive."

Following his instructions, I took time to examine the cave and recognized it as the same cave which I had seen in my long-ago vision.

Hearing my thoughts, he explained, "It is the same cave. Our mother knew it would be easier for you to speak with me in this familiar environment because your memories are embedded in the cells of the walls."

"Every time you introduce a topic, I find it difficult not to go down that line of thinking. For example, when you mention the cells of the cave picking up my memories, I want to discuss that…despite being eager to see your world firsthand."

"This occurs for several reasons," Jake explained. "Dragons receive information not only from their mothers and ancestors but also from the memories of the minerals in their hatching caves. Therefore, much of what I tell you is intuitively known by dragons. It is infused into our bodies as a known. These memories are food for us that we absorb from our time as an egg to the time we fledge. The aliveness of the stones that form this cave hold memories of me, my ancestors, and of you being here."

"Seeing as you're already discussing 'our' cave, could you say a bit more about how dragon dwellings hold memories of the inhabitants?" I asked, wanting to understand the process dragons used to instill memories in eggs and hatchlings.

"Each lineage uses specific caves for generations, so the minerals in the walls and floor are alive with the memories of those who have lived in them. A different dragon lineage would never consider living in a cave of another lineage. We are territorial and solitary beings. You have cats in your world who are mostly solitary, and we are like them. We would never consider visiting a cave of another lineage, or even the cave of one of our lineage, without first of all sending a telepathic request to see if this was acceptable. This is why each of our dwellings holds memories specific to individual dragons."

As he spoke, I examined the cave I'd seen in my vision to find out if I could pick up memories from the ancestors who lived here. Memories stirred in me but flew by quicker than I could remember them. Closing my eyes, I went deeper. At once, I was back in my first, long-ago vision when I saw dragon legs and, to my left, the egg of a dragon. Rather than fleeing this experience, as I'd done before, I stayed with it and watched the shell of the egg begin to crack.

Turning towards the mother dragon, I examined her fully for the first time. She was larger than Jake and darker in color… indigo that was almost black. With wise eyes, she watched the egg crack, but did not move forward to help. I understood that the hatchling had to be strong enough to survive on his own.

A wet straggly dragon emerged. Smiling, I recognized Jake… not that he looked the same… but he felt the same. He raised his scrawny neck and gazed intently into his mother's dark amber eyes, and I both felt and saw her download her memories in the form of images to him. Neither moved as this occurred. Finally, exhausted, he closed his eyes. It was only then that she moved close and, opening her lighter blue wings, placed them over him, warming him, even as a newborn chick is kept warm by the mother hen.

Knowing she was observed, she turned towards me and acknowledged my presence. I sensed no animosity and knew she approved of me witnessing the hatching process.

"Shall I share my memories with you, nestling?" she telepathically asked me. Her voice was both more powerful and more compassionate than that of my fledgling brother.

"I would like that if my brain is configured in a way you can do it?" I replied, knowing my human body could not be more different from her dragon one.

"This has nothing to do with your physical brain," she smiled, amused. "Mind exists outside space and time and our minds speak together."

Reassured, I focused on her eyes like I had witnessed Jake do. Her intense amber eyes magnetically held mine. She was so powerful it would have been impossible to break the link. For a split second, totally out of control, I panicked. Warm feelings of love and compassion flooded me and I understood her acceptance of me, a human, her willingness to brood me, and, more than that, her desire to share her ancestral lineage.

Opening to receive her ancestral memories, I felt as if I was plugged into a living computer, one that was downloading into my consciousness. From their earliest times, I saw the indigo dragons evolve their gifts of magic, deep knowing, and transmutation both in their world and then, as they journeyed to the stars where they assisted other races in developing consciousness. Receiving this living memory infusion, I felt no fear, only gratitude. I knew that she and her ancestors had consciously planned to create my nest brother to help our human race and that, even more, she had chosen to brood me in the dragon world. As yet, I was still unsure exactly how she'd done that, but, as Jake had requested, I put that question on hold until the knowledge easily awakened in my consciousness.

Completing the download, my brood mother released her magnetic hold and, giving me one last glance of approval, vanished. Speechless, I found myself back in the present moment with Jake who, once again, was both the size and age with which I was familiar.

He waited for me to recover from the intensity of the experience before speaking, "I hope you appreciate the honor that our mother has bestowed in giving you our ancestral memories. We never share our memories outside our lineage. She has done this because, for dragons, it's the most direct way to share accurate information."

Finding my voice, I replied, "I'm stunned because I didn't remember this experience. I never saw anything but her legs in my long-ago waking dream. Why is that?"

"You weren't ready to remember at that time. However, this memory was placed in you to gestate and to prepare you to return to our dragon world now. More and more, you are awakening to your true birthright and all will become known in time."

"Do you grow into the ancestral memories that are downloaded into you at birth?" I asked, following my intuitive hunch.

"Absolutely," my dragon brother answered, before adding, "And so do you."

The light went on. "I've always known that each of us has a cell, something I refer to as the 'unicell', that stores information by our soul. This information is unlocked and becomes available to use as our frequency rises during our life. I've always assumed our soul would download only what was necessary for our specific purpose in any given life. I've never seen myself living in the dragon world which, let's face it, would be impossible as a human."

"Your problem is that you've made an incorrect assumption. You are so attached to your current physical human form that you cannot imagine anything different."

"True; yet, that being said, the problem remains. I'm a human and you're a dragon and your world is made for dragons. How will I be able to explore it?"

I rose from my chair and walked to the entrance of the cave. Looking down, I saw that we were hundreds of feet in the air. Jake came and stood beside me. I wasn't certain if this felt reassuring or more precarious. I've never been a fan of heights and there were many more locations I would rather be. Also, I had no idea how he was going to take me around his world. Clearly, walking was out and I didn't see any helicopters emerging for my convenience.

Letting me anxiously stew for a minute, he finally said, "You have two choices. Either I take you on my back, or you visualize yourself with a dragon body and fly with me."

"Do you have any saddles and reins here?" I asked, remembering that dragon riders in fantasy books rode in this way... safely.

"Of course not," he replied, squinting his eyes in disapproval at my suggestion.

"So much for option one. What is option three?" I asked as I had no clue how to turn myself into a dragon.

"There is no option three."

Back to the only remaining option, I asked, "Okay, how do I turn myself into a flying dragon? What tools...?"

"No tools. Just do it," he said, cutting off my question. "Focus on what our brood mother and I look like and imagine yourself in a dragon body. This is the way others who visit our world do it.

And ... a word of advice. Make sure you imagine yourself our size. We will meet other dragons and we don't want to be conspicuous. I recommend you practice today and be prepared to travel when you return tomorrow."

Jake and the cave disappeared, and I found myself back in my meditation garden. The homework assignment was not desirable, but he'd made it clear that I'd best do it, and do it well, or there would be no excursions in the dragon world. This ultimatum was a great motivator to immediately start practicing.

I began by visualizing our dragon mother because she and I were both female. Because she was older, she was larger than my partially grown fledgling brother. Also, I knew inside myself that dragon females were larger than males. Visualizing a dragon body was surprisingly easy, but I was stumped by my color. To see my color, I'd have to look at myself from the outside; however, I was reluctant to give up being in my dragon body. As a dragon, I felt large, powerful, confident, and I wanted to fully explore it. Unfortunately, because I doubted my ability to maintain a dragon body, I lost my focus and found myself back in my human body. Disappointed, I tried again to imagine myself as a dragon and it worked. Pushing aside a desire to see my color, I congratulated myself on my success and decided I'd accomplished enough to satisfy Jake.

Dragon Lineages

Walking to the garden bench the next day, the pressure was on. Would I be able to create a dragon body to go to the dragon world? I repeated what I had done the previous evening by visualizing myself as a large, female indigo-black dragon. In other words, I copied what my brood mother looked like.

Starting with talons, I imagined them muscled with large sharp nails, and, working up my scaled legs, I made them identical to the pillars I'd first seen many years ago in the cave. I examined my belly and saw it was plump and rounded, much fatter than the slender torso I had as a human. After all, if I was going to be a dragon, I might as well give myself the body I wished. Now for the rest of my body. Dark indigo, almost black, seemed right. Oops... green and rose infiltrated my indigo image and mostly settled under my wings that were beautiful and delicate, but strong enough to support my deliciously plump body. Finally, I looked at my eyes. They were golden with a black iris and, somewhat disappointed, I saw my human image reflected in them. Darn, was I doing something wrong?

Reviewing my appearance, I was pleasantly relieved that my dragon image was holding. I congratulated myself and decided it was good enough to present to Jake. And call me a brat, but I was happy that I would be larger than him. Focusing intently on holding my dragon shape, I mentally projected myself into the cave and landed beside Jake.

Rising to his full height, he walked around me checking to make sure I'd replaced all my human parts with those of a dragon. Returning to face me, he looked into my eyes and smiled, "Well done. Very impressive."

"Thanks," I said. "However, I've discovered that my human body is reflected in my eyes, whereas your eyes reflect a dragon body."

"That's normal. Don't worry about it. Dragons will always know you are a human if they look in your eyes. It can't be helped and most dragons won't mind that you're a human taking on a dragon body. Actually, my fledgling companions will be both amused and curious about you."

"Are we going to meet them?" I asked anxiously. One dragon seemed enough to me.

"Yes we will, but before we leave the cave you need to understand about our various dragon lineages. This will help you to recognize other dragons and identify their gifts if, the Source be with us, an old one might address you."

"That's a perfect way to start," I acknowledged, crouching beside him.

"Each dragon lineage is dominant on one of the rays of energy and their color indicates their chief gift, power, and soul frequency. All beings, even humans, have a dominant soul energy indicated by a particular ray. When you meet any dragon, you will notice that he, or she, has a dominant color and other minor colors."

"Yes, I see that you have various colors. Can you explain what they mean?"

"Look at me," he said, standing up and extending his wings. "My dominant color is indigo, but my chest and belly contain many blue hues and even hints of green. And my wings, if you look closely, have flecks of red."

As Jake spoke, he flexed his wings so I could see glimpses of red and, as he swayed from one leg to the other, I noticed various blue and green tones.

"Now let's examine your colors, Tanis," he said, studying me. "You are mostly indigo like me, but darker because you are older in human years and I am younger in dragon age.

"Lift your wings?" he said and I did as he directed. "As I thought, you have a lot of green and rose hidden under your wings."

"I wouldn't say 'hidden,'" I interrupted, taking offense. "Anyway, what do these colors mean?"

"Let's start with indigo as this is both your and my dominant color and lineage. We receive this lineage from our mother. Indigo, as we've said, is the color of magic and transmutation and these are our gifts. Members of my lineage make sure that there are a lot of crystals embedded in the structures of our caves that help to catalyze transmutation. Dragons choose caves that reflect and assist with their specific gifts."

"And what about my green and rose colors?" I asked.

He became silent and examined me with piercing eyes. I felt deeply assessed and knew he was waiting for me to be in the best possible frequency before he continued.

"I have an idea. I think it would be better for you to meet dragons with different gifts to learn what their colors mean from them."

"I'd like to meet your fledgling friends, but please not old dragons. Am I ready now?" I looked forward to seeing the dragon world for myself, but still, I confess, I was nervous about meeting more dragons.

He closed his eyes and went inward and I felt him sending a telepathic message. A moment later, opening his eyes, he said, "I've asked my friends to join us at our meeting place. I could teleport you, but that takes a lot of energy. Are you able to fly with me?"

As he spoke, he walked towards the cave entrance and expected me to follow, which I did. Looking out from the entrance I saw that we were many hundreds of feet in the air with a steep drop.

"What about a test flight inside the cave?" I suggested, uncertain about my ability.

"Follow my lead and we'll go slow," he said, leaping into the air.

Fanning my wings several times to build up courage, I lifted off the cliff. 'Don't look down. Don't look down,' I kept saying to myself as I pumped my wings. To my relief, I discovered that I was not losing elevation and was flying more or less level. The secret seemed to be to allow my dragon body to do what it was built for and not to think about it. At that moment, Jake pulled up beside me and, nodding encouragement, directed my attention to the far hills.

"That's where we'll meet the others," he sent the thought into my mind. "They realize you are a human and will be tolerant of your idiosyncrasies."

"What idiosyncrasies?" I asked. I had no idea what he meant and wanted to make a good impression by eliminating impediments.

"This desire to please is one of the idiosyncrasies. Dragons don't care about this. It's a human trait, I'd say weakness because it wastes energy better spent doing exactly what you feel called to do. Anyway, we're almost there. I'd suggest that you don't say anything and let me do the introductions."

Jake was all business now and it dawned on me that his peers would judge his project of teaching the human based on how I performed. I was so proud of my natural flying ability as a dragon that I decided meeting his friends couldn't be that bad. Deciding to be on my best behavior, I stared straight ahead as we approached the hills.

He slowed and hovered above a plateau located in a circular bowl surrounded by mountains. Looking down, I saw dragons of many different colors raising their heads to check us out. Jake landed a little away from the dragon cluster and I appreciated that he wanted to give me space for my first-ever landing. Thinking of how airplanes raise their wing flaps when they land, I made a beautiful landing and, once again, gave myself a mental 'high-five'. Still, unlike the fledglings, I didn't feel secure in my dragonness yet.

"Hello, hello," said an attractive green dragon waddling towards us.

"This is a special day when a human comes to meet us," he said, bobbing his head and grinning as only dragons can grin exposing his foot-long teeth.

Not certain of the correct protocol, I bobbed my head back at him.

"Tanis," my dragon brother said, "meet Hisssflllummm." Dragon names were clearly not meant for human voice I thought to myself as Jake hissed and hummed the green dragon's name. "As you see, his lineage is emerald and he'll explain what that means."

While my brother spoke, the other dragons stayed where they were. They seemed to sense that I could only handle meeting one new dragon at a time and knew their turn would come.

The green dragon, still smiling, began, "Green dragon colors can be anything from a lime green to a mint green and we may even have an autumn green in our wings and a sage green in our upper body. As you observe, I'm spring green, but I'll probably darken to emerald as I get older. That's usually what happens."

The young dragon gazed at Jake and mentally nudged him asking if I was clever enough to understand what he'd said.

Jake started laughing and responded, "She understands everything and you're lucky she's not bombarding you with questions."

Was that a signal for me to start talking, I wondered? Yet, before I could speak to the green dragon to let him know I was intelligent, my dragon brother gave me a strong 'NO' message.

"Hahaha!" the green dragon laughed, picking up our interchange. "I see what you mean."

"Tell her your gifts," urged my brother.

"Most storytellers are emerald dragons," Hisssflllummm began, "because we have a lighter, more curious, and not such a serious frequency, and we retain our inner youth in a way that perhaps other lineages don't. Of course, elders in all lineages are storytellers because they can speak about their lineages, ancestry, and from their deep personal knowledge. However, the emerald lineage is particularly good at telling stories of individual dragons who have been a bit unique. They tell these stories for entertainment, but they are also teaching lessons. We use a light, humorous approach whereas indigo dragons would be more didactic."

"Could I interrupt and ask a question?" I requested when he paused to take a breath. "On my planet, Earth, we often associate the color green with the plant world. I'm wondering if dragons have gardens, plants, and trees, and, if so, is the emerald lineage in-volved with them?"

"That's a good question," he replied. "I hadn't thought about that. Hmmm … Hmmm… We've studied your planet and, from what I've learned, our world is more arid. It's more mountainous and our mountains are higher. Our oceans are deeper too. Our environment is more dramatic, more extreme in everything. Hmmm … Hmmm… Some areas have very tall trees and plants, but these are relatively few. We don't think much about plants. We're more into minerals and our world has plenty of those."

Hisssflllummm looked at my dragon brother in approval and mentally asked him a question. Jake nodded and the green dragon turned to me and said, "I know you're good at giving nicknames; I'd like one too."

Nicknames seemed to be the latest dragon craze, and I was pleased to oblige. Closing my eyes, I focused on his cheery, chatty personality, and received the perfect name.

"Kenny," I replied. "This name makes me think of Ireland and, on my planet, Ireland is nicknamed the emerald isle."

"Kenny, it is," he acknowledged smiling.

Turning around, he walked back to join the others at the same time as a ruby-red dragon walked forward to claim his time. I became wary as he approached and stepped back. He was taller and broader than the other fledglings and exuded immense fire energy.

"Don't be afraid of me," he said in a deep bass voice. "Being human, you associate red with being bellicose, but ruby dragons don't have this quality. For us, red is the color of warmth and energy."

He turned his head towards the other dragons as he spoke and they nodded in agreement.

Swinging back to me, he continued, "We ruby dragons have a variety of colors ranging from a yellow-orange, through crimson to a dark red, almost mahogany. Our colors reflect the colors of the sun. Our gift is warmth and other lineages seek us for that purpose."

I must have looked vacant because the ruby dragon interrupted and decided to give an example with which I could relate.

"We have different seasons in our world, much as you do on Earth," the ruby dragon explained. "In seasons of energy, something like your summer, ruby dragons are particularly energized in finding minerals and crystals and making these available to other dragons for food and for many uses, and in the winter season dragons gather in a larger communal area to listen to stories. Dragons usually prefer to not have other dragons near them, however, they want to be near us because we radiate warmth and energy. When you humans move beyond your bellicose feelings, you will no longer associate red with warlike qualities, but more as a form of energy."

His last comments stung, which may not have been his intention, as ruby dragons seemed to be direct. In any event, finished, he walked back towards the others and nodded to a sapphire-blue dragon encouraging her to speak with me. The sapphire dragon, exuding calm and peace, took her time walking forward.

"As you can observe," she said slowly by way of introduction, "I'm mostly the color of the sky. Our lineage ranges from very light blue, almost white, all the way to navy. We could have a few flecks of different colors that we've inherited from other lineages, however, the sapphires have the purest dragon lineage. We're the least likely to breed with other dragons as we wish to keep our lineage pure."

Turning towards the ruby and emerald dragons, she added, not without humor, "Sometimes a sapphire sire is asked to breed with a ruby or emerald dam to calm the hatchlings being born in that lineage."

The ruby and emerald dragons smiled and didn't take offense demonstrating that this was an old joke with them about their differences.

Returning her attention to me, the sapphire dragon continued, "We have chosen for countless generations to move into inner planes. In your terms, we are the meditative, spiritual ones. We are more interested in the inner world, rather than the outer world. We seldom travel to other worlds, or even in our own world, unless we are needed. Sometimes sapphire blue dragons are needed to calm either dragons who are having a dispute, or throwbacks who may be saved if they could learn to control their emotions. We calm other dragons not by talking, but by radiating peaceful stillness."

"Could you give an example of what dragons would have a dispute about in your world?" I asked, relieved to hear that humans were not the only ones having disputes.

"Okay, I'll give an example," she said, happy to share. "Dragons might occasionally have a heated discussion about ways that our evolution should advance. Some might wish to advance more quickly in a direction that others would consider dangerous. At such a time, a sapphire dragon would sit in these discussions so that all dragons could enter a more meditative, still place to discover what path the Source of All desired. Our differences are caused because of the filter our various lineages use, rather than how advanced we are in evolution. We are an evolving race and are still not perfected."

"It's the same for humans," I interrupted, attempting to show similarities between our races. "Depending on our parental and cultural upbringing, we may want very different things."

The sapphire dragon withdrew into herself and I realized she had spoken more than she usually did. Mentally, and with a slight smile, she asked me if she too could have a nickname. It was a privilege to do so as she exuded peace and both inner and outer beauty. Closing my eyes, I relaxed into her beautiful aura and her name emerged."

"Your nickname is Grace," I said. "Do you like it?"

"Oh, yes," she replied. "Grace is ideal. What does it mean?"

"In my world the name Grace signifies one who is blessed and others feel blessed to be with her."

As I spoke, the other dragons nodded in agreement at her name.

One rainbow-colored dragon remained and I had no idea what lineage it was. As it approached, I noticed that it, like the sapphire-blue dragon, was a female. She smiled at my dragon brother as she approached and I caught something like 'thank you for bringing her' in the message she sent.

Bending towards me, she said, "We rainbow-hued dragons are caretakers, healers who specialize in working with our throwbacks on various worlds. We have a little bit of ruby, sapphire, emerald, and indigo depending on the lineages with which we specialize. Hmmm ... There is more variety in the caretaker lineage than the other lineages because throwbacks can be of many lineages. The caretaker lineage specializes in healing and nurturing throwbacks and those who are borderline and still living in our world. We teach these dragons how to calm their emotions to be copacetic with other dragons. Rainbow dragons spend at least 50 percent of their time in other worlds. When we return to our homeworld, we rest to recharge and sometimes work with young dragons. There are more rainbow-hued dragons than any other lineage."

"Two questions are going through my mind," I said to her.

"And the first one is…," she acknowledged indulgently.

"Why are there more rainbow dragons?"

"Isn't it obvious?" she asked, not expecting an answer. "Long ago dragons didn't breed for specific qualities. We bred with individual dragons that we liked. That was a time when we dwelled in lower astral frequencies and, therefore, were more emotional. Then, most dragons were mixtures of lineages. Now we try to keep our lineages relatively pure, but, as you observe, I, being of the rainbow lineage, have all colors."

"Are rainbow dragons treated as lesser than pure lineage dragons?" I asked, going into risky territory.

"Not at all. We are now regarded as a pure lineage and we interbreed to continue this tradition. One of our gifts, in addition to healing, is that we are more flexible than the other lineages because we are composed of so many lineages."

"Second question…?" she invited.

"I'm wondering if you have yellow dragons?"

"No. Yellow is a tone of our ruby dragons," interjected the larger, ruby-red male.

"That's correct," acknowledged the rainbow-hued female, before adding, "I'd like a nickname too… if you don't mind?"

It was the first time a dragon had thought of my comfort, and I felt that consideration for others was one of her gifts. Closing my eyes, I saw her many rainbow hues dancing to her heartbeat and her name came.

"Beth," I shared, opening my eyes.

"Perfect," she smiled.

"I'd like a nickname too," said the ruby dragon, stepping forth. "I should have asked you earlier."

"That's easy," I replied. "Grant. It's a forthright name and you are that."

"I accept," replied Grant, and, in a flash, I saw his strength and the leader he would become.

"Are there white dragons because I don't see any here?" I requested, addressing my dragon brother, who had been patiently waiting for his fellow fledglings to have their turn with the human.

"Something would be terribly wrong if this happened," Jake replied, moving his head from side to side and looking at the other dragons as to how to proceed. They cast their eyes down making it clear that he was on his own to answer my question.

"White does not indicate purity in our world," he continued. "It indicates emptiness and being without a lineage. A white dragon would not be nurtured. Oh, I see this idea is repellent to you. Our laws and your laws are not necessarily the same. If a dragon is empty and has no lineage, how can he, or she, learn and grow? It's not just that the color is missing; it's that the personality is missing. A white dragon would not be cared for and sometimes one of our dragons of peace would go and stay with it until it died."

He glanced towards the other dragons to see if any of them wanted to add anything. Beth, the rainbow female, stepped in.

"We usually would know before that dragon hatched that there was a serious problem and it would not be brooded. This is very rare. It could occur when the sire or the dam were too young. They should not have been breeding because they couldn't pass on their lineage or ancestral information. Hmmm…Hmmm… In our world breeding isn't just a physical act of passing on genetic material, it's an act of thought, and two young dragons, such as myself, would never consider doing this. However, sometimes there can be an error in judgment with very young dragons, which is rare, but it can happen. Then this kind of defect can occur in the egg."

"Thank you for explaining," I replied, "because it helps me to be more accepting of your decision. As you say, humans are a different race with different laws."

Although each dragon was very helpful, I was exhausted and my dragon body began to revert to its human form. Jake noticed the change and said, "We've covered the major lineages. That's it for today. Return to your world and we'll speak tomorrow."

At once I found myself back in my meditation garden safe on Earth. I was exhilarated to have flown and to have met so many dragons, but it was a great drain on my mind as well as body. I needed to completely change my wiring to be in a dragon body, which was doubly difficult from being in my human body in their high-frequency world. Still, having done it once, I was confident that I could do it again…tomorrow.

Fledgling School

As dawn was breaking, Grant, the young ruby dragon, appeared in my inner vision. "Put on your dragon body and come now," he commanded in his deep voice. "It's time for school."

I found it curious that Grant, rather than my dragon brother, would contact me. However, I assumed there was a good reason and decided to heed the call. Sitting in my meditation room at home, I imagined creating my dragon body. As I had previously, I visualized myself as a dragon by modeling myself on the image of my brood mother, but I added subtle differences in my coloring this time.

Completing the transformation, I reached out to the dragon world with my inner sight and saw the group of fledglings waiting for me in the same location where I'd met them before. But Jake was not among them.

"Where's Jake?" I asked. I found it unlike him to leave me alone when I was so new to the dragon world and his friends.

"He's waiting for us at the learning place," answered Grant, who had taken on leadership.

Beth interrupted, "I'm not certain this is a good idea."

"What idea?" I inquired anxiously.

"Jake suggested we take you to school with us, but the master may not appreciate it," responded Beth. I could tell she was the responsible one, a gift of the rainbow lineage, which I was happy to follow.

"It will be lots of fun," urged Kenny when he saw me hesitate. "Come on, let's go!"

They turned to look at me as one. Beth shrugged her shoulders admitting defeat since the other three were sending me encouraging messages. I nodded agreement and, surrounded by fledgling dragons, rose into the air. Grant took the lead and Kenny pulled up beside him jostling him and laughing. Grace and Beth, on either side of me, sent a good-humored 'silly boys' message to each other that I intercepted. It was wonderful to be among their contagious youthful energy, and I put my anxiety on hold as we flew higher into the mountains.

Being a dragon was exhilarating and I felt proud of myself that I could keep up with them in flight. I loved pumping my strong wings and gliding through the air. I was free and powerful in my dragon body and would have preferred to continue exploring their world, but it was not to be. Cresting a particularly high peak, we emerged over a flat plateau. At one end stood a large, sapphire dragon flicking his tail from side to side. The fledglings immediately became serious and Kenny dropped back and whispered to me, "Oops. We're late."

Circling the basin, we descended as a group and landed at the far side. The fledglings surrounded me one in front, one behind, and two on either side. Why were they trying to keep me out of sight? Recalling Beth's warning, I began thinking this outing was a very, very bad idea.

The massive male dragon moved towards us at the same time as Jake popped up on my left side and, throwing his wing over me, pulled me closer.

"Sorry to be late, master," said Kenny, exuding charm.

"And why are you?" commanded the large blue dragon in a booming voice.

Beth, trying to rescue the situation, replied, "We have no excuse. We were dawdling."

"Yes, dawdling," echoed Grant. Grace nodded as did the other fledglings and I heard them send apologetic messages towards their teacher.

Understandably curious to see why the fledglings were huddled together, the master continued his approach.

I closed my eyes and wanted to disappear.

"No. Stay!" murmured my dragon brother, pulling me even nearer with his wing.

As the huge sapphire dragon drew near, Grant moved aside. So did Beth. Then Grace. Finally, Kenny gave way until my dragon sibling was left exposed with his wing outstretched over me as I, shaking, huddled underneath.

"What have we here?" demanded the master. "Jaakelousekindvron have you brought a hatchling to class?"

Jake's heart was beating fast and mine was galloping along with it.

"Let's see, Jaakelousekindvron. Remove your wing."

Jake did as ordered, leaving me crouching and exposed.

"So. Not a nestling, but a human in a dragon body. Where did you get it?"

"Hmmm … Hmmm … I've been talking to her. She's my … Hmmm … well, it's like this, Sir — my nest sister."

"Enough!" the teacher ordered Jake.

"Come!" he commanded, peering at me. With those words, he turned around and marched forward.

Doing as he instructed, I followed reluctantly.

"Turn around!" he ordered when I reached the front. I was in his territory with his rules, so I obeyed his command without hesitating.

Staring at the fledglings, the teacher said, "This is an excellent opportunity to study a human."

I felt naked in my dragon body and my concentration started to waver followed by a wavering of my dragon form.

"How do we know it's a human?" the master asked, turning towards Grant.

"Well, look at how her body is flickering," he replied, giving me an apologetic look for bringing me.

"If it wasn't wavering, if its concentration was better, how would you know?" he threw the question in Grace's direction.

"By looking in the eyes," answered Grace, giving me a 'What can I do?' look.

"Yes, but if you hadn't seen its eyes, Jaakelousekindvron, how would you know?" the teacher demanded.

"She smells different," murmured my dragon brother, sending me an embarrassed glance.

I was not pleased to discover that I smelled different, but I didn't have time to think about this as the master was hot on my trail.

"If you weren't close enough to smell it, or to see its eyes, and, if it was more skilled at holding its dragon form, how would you know?"

They were all silent. The dragon master smiled, thoroughly pleased that his question had stumped them. I, on the other hand, was becoming increasingly annoyed at being called 'it'.

"I know," volunteered Kenny. "She's more sensitive than us and shows her emotions on her skin."

"That's correct," said the master. "It hasn't the same control of its mind as we dragons."

"That's enough," I interrupted. "I'm not an 'it'; I'm a 'she.'"

"Ah!" he laughed. "It talks."

"Of course, I talk." I raised my voice and stared up at him.

He looked at me with curiosity. Without asking permission, he dove into my mind to discover my level of intelligence. I felt him descend deeper and deeper into who I was, what I was, and why I was in the dragon world. Questions, questions. I became an open book, revealed and read by him.

"He's a scholar," I thought. He pulled back surprised that I'd noticed both his inner nature and his deep desire to convey the accumulated knowledge of his life to the young fledglings.

"Is it normal for sapphire dragons to teach fledglings?" I asked now that I had his attention.

He paused and I could hear the wheels turning as he wondered if answering or not answering my question would result in the most information for his students.

"Answering would perhaps ensure my cooperation," I sent this thought strongly to him as I didn't want him to continue treating me as a thing.

He heard me loud and clear and responded, "We sapphires have more patience with the young ones. And there can be teachers in other lineages."

"Would you mind taking your human form so we could examine it?" he asked, cashing in on my promise to cooperate. Although he was courteous, which was a definite improvement, I'd had enough of being treated like a specimen. He was easily twice my size, but my justified annoyance caused him to pause to consider a strategy to gain my compliance.

"You're obviously here to learn from dragons and we're here today to learn from you. Why not exchange information?" he replied, sending waves of calm over me.

"Very well," I capitulated and allowed my dragon body to dissolve. The fledglings gasped and started chattering among themselves when they saw my human form. Jake, trying to protect me, sent them a disapproving look and they took the hint and went outwardly silent. What they didn't count on was that I could hear their inner thoughts as easily as a human as I could as a dragon.

"If she can become a dragon, then maybe I could become a human," Beth thought, flashing her rainbow scales, eager to try something new.

"She's got strange scales," thought Kenny, evidently not looking closely enough to discover that my clothes weren't scales.

They moved closer to examine me and Grant, always the first to try something, reached out and touched my arm. "Look at how fragile she is," he exclaimed. "Touch her."

"I can hear you, Grant. I'm still the same in my consciousness and, if others are going to touch, be gentle and one at a time."

In my human form, the fledglings were much larger and my body was vulnerable and, let's not forget, they were young and unpredictable as evidenced by them bringing me into this uncomfortable situation.

"I'll be gentle," said Grace, picking up on my unease. She gently reached out and laid one sharp talon on my arm while looking at my eyes to see if it was okay."

It felt strange in my human body to be touched by a dragon. Although her talon didn't scratch me, I was only too aware of its power to grasp and pierce my skin. Grace noticed my discomfort and pulled back.

I wouldn't mind feeling the whiskers on your head," Kenny asked me. "Is that permitted?"

"I started to laugh and Jake joined in as he was much more familiar with human anatomy than his friends.

"Silly," he said to Kenny. "That's hair. All humans have it."

"Yeah. Go ahead," I replied to Kenny who immediately stepped forward and started combing my hair carefully with his talons.

"This is nice," he asserted and, turning to his friends, continued, "Come here. Try this."

One by one, each stepped forward to stroke my hair. It resembled hair brushing and I enjoyed it. Sensing my pleasure, they moved into resonance with me and started to softly hum together.

"That's enough. You don't want to hurt her," interrupted the massive male dragon, urging them to stop. Although he attempted to be serious, I knew he was resisting humming himself because, after all, he was the teacher.

I was pleased to have been of use as a teaching aid and asked him, "Is this the usual way dragons learn here? Do you learn from live specimens?"

"I usually teach telepathically," the master replied, sending me a holographic image of himself standing in front of the class of fledglings. Closing off the image, he continued, "Yet, it's wonderful to have a live specimen to view."

Jake realized I was tired and said, "Sir, I think she's had enough."

"Yes," the master acknowledged, noticing my slumped shoulders. "Do you want to take her back to her homeworld and we'll continue ourselves?"

"That's not necessary," Jake stated and his tone conveyed his pride in me.

"Oh, she can go by herself. Good," replied the teacher.

Turning to me, he continued, "When you arrive home, send us a telepathic picture of your homeworld so we can see it."

Nodding goodbye to my new fledgling friends, I instantly returned to my home and walked outside. Looking out over the ocean, I sent a telepathic link back to them of what I was observing. They could see the gulls flying, the seals swimming in the water, and an eagle diving for a fish. They were impressed and interested in what they saw and the master sent me a thank you message.

"I'm pleased to be of service," I respectfully answered and closed the link.

All turned out well in the end and the teacher seemed pleased with the fledglings' initiative. Witnessing Jake relating with other dragons, I noticed that he was protective of me and that he appeared more mature than the other fledglings. Even Grant deferred to him and none of them, unlike Jake, had left their dragon world yet. By taking me to meet his friends, Jake was not bragging, but was attempting to include them in his experiences. Because the fledglings were approximately the same age, I wondered why he was allowed to work with me when they were only in training. Whatever the reason, I was grateful that he was taking me around his world and introducing me to so many interesting encounters and beings.

The Old Water Dragon

Several days elapse. Days turn into weeks. Still, I do not return to the dragon world. Am I too tired? Partially, and partially it seems like too much effort. The time isn't right. I'm not ready. Perhaps it's the dark of the moon. Perhaps it's mercury retrograde. Perhaps it's too much going on in my day-to-day life. But I don't want to press forward. I don't want to strain. Instead, I want to do everything with joy and ease. I know this is a lesson for me and I'm sure my dragon brother and all the great masters would agree. It doesn't matter if others think I'm lazy when I'm in a being, rather than a doing, state. I am learning to abstain from both internal and external pressures to always move forward instead of remaining in the present moment.

And what has this to do with dragons and the dragon world? Perhaps this message is not immediately obvious, but this attitude to which I refer is how we access higher frequencies. This is how we can journey to the realms where the elementals, angels, masters, and dragons exist. We can speak with them and be with them by not pressuring ourselves. Yes, granted, we must use our will, persistence, and determination to access higher frequencies, but these qualities need to be balanced with meditation, contemplation, and an inner sense of rightness about appropriate timing.

Therefore, one day I sit down quietly, meditatively, and ask if the time is right to return to the dragon world. I hear my dragon brother say 'yes' and this 'yes' I feel inside me as an inner knowing that I have unlimited free will. I discover that I have free will to respond to the 'yes' and I can move this 'yes' around, depending on how much I value it and if I want to implement it, and I find it interesting to practice doing this. I have no boundaries and play with the 'yes'. Through this exploration, I learn deeper lessons about higher astral frequencies and perceive that this learning might be useful for humans at this time.

I feel as if, by sharing himself and his world, Jake is dangling bait in front of curious humans to want to read his story. In doing so, they are captured like fish on a line into the deeper knowing and higher frequency of his world, which is what he desires. If we eat the bait that's being dangled, each of us can go to his world ourselves. The story, as he said, is only to create a pathway, a bridge, and to suggest to humans that this is possible for them as well.

Once I absorbed his message, I began to prepare myself to take on a dragon body so I could travel around his world. It wasn't easy which reminded me of what it's like to get dressed up when you haven't worn certain clothes for a long time. After I finally succeeded, I decided to travel through space instead of teleporting to the dragon world. My decision was born from a growing confidence that I could explore and experiment more than I had previously thought. Deep space was dark…empty…yet not empty. There was an intelligent consciousness in everything and organizing everything. By aligning myself with this pulse of consciousness, my subtle desire to go to the dragon world was heard. Immediately I was there in the cave but, this time, Jake was not on hand to greet me. Did he not know I was coming? Will he return and, if so, when? My questions were like a soft impulse before having a thought. They were only curiosities, not desires.

I wandered around the cave and discovered that it was much larger than I had previously thought. Now as I explored the deep recesses of the cave, I saw the walls lined with rubies, sapphires, emeralds, and crystals. My dragon eyes saw not only the surface of these gems but also what lay beneath the surface. With deeper sight, I realized that this cave was chosen by my brood mother to use gems and crystals for energization and that similar caves existed throughout the dragon world for the same purpose.

I saw that dragons were created by their crystal environment much as humans were created by the abundant water environment of Earth. I discovered that my dragon body was not as watery as my human body and that systems of conscious crystals had replaced my human organs. Why? Because in the higher-frequency dragon world, physical organs were not necessary. Instead, dragons had evolved mental and spiritual organs to travel both through and outside space and time.

I realized that caretaker dragons took these gems to the throwbacks on Earth both for food and to help to heal the throwbacks. I understood how very difficult it was for the throwbacks to live in the watery environment of Earth, which was so different from their arid world. At that moment, I sensed Jake returning to the cave, so I quickly withdrew my attention from the gems and crystals and moved to join him.

He was happy to see me. He didn't need to smile or embrace me, as humans would, for me to know this. Instead, his energy hummed in a way that indicated happiness.

"Hmmm… You've been learning about our gems and crystals and how their vibratory fields helped us to develop a flowing unity of thought and consciousness," Jake said when he saw what I'd been doing.

"What I've observed is that dragons use gems and crystals to enter what humans refer to as synchronous oscillation," I commented. "This occurs when our brain moves into a coherent pattern which is most often found in deep meditative states. By doing this, we move into higher frequencies which resemble your harmonic humming."

"Yes, there are similarities," Jake replied, "but dragons employ the crystal-like organs of our body to resonate with the Source of All."

"Speaking of crystals, I've been wondering if they help you to produce fire."

"Absolutely. Crystals in our stomachs allow us to breathe a transmuting and transforming fire of consciousness."

The light went on and I remembered that in an earlier conversation, Jake had mentioned that humans, as we evolve, will have more crystal-like properties in our cells. Clearly, clarification was necessary.

"Does this mean that humans will also be able to breathe fire in the future?" I said excited by the prospect.

"Hahaha. That's funny. No this is a dragon gift and one you don't need. Humans will be able to use their fire through their hands to manifest and demanifest form, also through their eyes. Certainly, you could have fire coming out of your mouth if you wanted, however, that's probably not what you'll use fire for as you will develop other uses for crystal in your cells and in your mind."

Eager to pursue this topic, I opened my mouth just in time to hear Jake say, "I prefer not to answer any more questions about fire.

Today I thought we could meet a dragon who lives in water and you can speak with him yourself."

His suggestion sounded exciting and I was easily persuaded. I'd come to trust his plans because I learned so much by doing so.

Sensing my agreement, he walked to the cave entrance and took flight. I followed him easily and was increasingly confident of my flying ability when he swerved to the left towards the fast-approaching mountain peaks. There was no time for a gradual ascent and we began climbing higher and higher until, finally, a cool air current supported us. From that height, we were able to glide with no effort and I hoped to enjoy this new experience for a long time but it was not to be. Jake quickly descended to a lower elevation and, following his lead, I looked and saw a great expanse of water. If it had been Earth, I would have guessed it was as large as the Mediterranean Sea.

Pulling up his outstretched wings, my brother landed on the sand and I flopped down, not as gracefully, beside him. Jake telepathically began calling to a being in the water to announce our arrival. Wrapped in the outer message was a second, polite inner message requesting an audience. Hearing his respectful inner message informed me that he was seeking an audience with an older, mature dragon. Standing on the shore near the water, my dragon brother assumed an erect posture. Following his lead, I did the same. Looking out to sea, I saw ripples moving towards us that quickly became larger waves as they neared the shore. An old, large dragon emerged sending waves up our legs to our belly and chest.

Looking only at Jake, the old dragon grumbled in annoyance. "I have heard your request and come. What do you want?"

"I have brought ….," began my brother in an apologetic tone.

"Yes, I see what you have brought. A human. And what do you want that you disturb my dreams?"

Jake sank into himself, then recovered and stood more fully erect. "I would not disturb your dreams wise one, if it were not important. This human is a messenger between her race and ours. We are meeting others in our world to teach her so that she can give this information to other humans. We beg, ask, request for your gift of water wisdom in order for your lineage to be represented among the teachings."

Until then, the old dragon had dismissed me with a glance. Now he turned and flooded me with piercing questions. He rapidly examined all my thoughts, emotions, motivations. In short, everything from top to bottom, inner and outer. In another circumstance, I might have been offended by this invasion but, in this situation, it seemed like a normal course of events. After all, why should he give us his time if it was of no benefit to him or his lineage? Through his deep sight, the water dragon concluded that the Source of All was in alignment with our request and he turned back to my dragon brother.

"Very well. You have my attention. What do you wish to ask?"

Until that moment, I'd been so intimidated by his size and physical differences from other dragons that I hadn't thoroughly examined him. Now I did. It's hard to say what his color was. He appeared to move from visibility to invisibility. To be here and not here. This must be what he meant when he said that we were keeping him from his dreams. In his dreams, he must become invisible to others.

Hearing my thoughts, the water dragon turned back towards me. He knew that I had correctly surmised what happened to him in his dream state when he moved out of bodily form into higher invisible realms. I knew by his look that he approved of my observation and he stood watching me while I examined him more deeply.

The crest on his head was much larger than that of my dragon brother and the other fledglings. It was ridged and not entirely solid and more flexible. His crest continued from his brow to the back of his head and somewhat down his neck. I had a hunch that his crest functioned as a receiving antenna for deep dreams. At my thought, he nodded and acknowledged my inner knowing. His legs were much shorter than those of land-based dragons and there were webs between each talon for swimming and propelling him through the water. His body was more streamlined and his tail was stronger than Jake's and had a larger rudder at the end to steer him through the water.

Turning back to my sibling, the old water dragon said, "I see now why you brought her. It's the first human I've met and perhaps I prejudged her race. Still, I have little time for questions. I'm drying out on the beach and wish to return to the depths. Be quick. What do you want to know?"

Jake turned to me and, nodding, encouraged me to ask questions. "Wise one," I began, sending a telepathic message of respect and gratitude for his attention, "I see that dreaming deep dreams are…"

That's as far as I got before the water dragon interrupted. "Your questions are too slow, let me tell you." With that comment he began sending me fast telepathic messages full of images to accompany his words and I simultaneously saw, felt, and heard his answer.

"Water dragons are deep dreamers. We are in the process of removing ourselves from the physical realm and becoming disembodied. Maintaining this physical body is an effort for us. We lie on the ocean floor in places of energy where we meditate, contemplate, and dream communally. Unlike land dragons, we tend to be communal at least for dreaming. Our dreams can extend for long periods of time during which we seek to move to higher, disembodied frequencies. We sing songs together. You could call them humming chants. We increase the opportunity for all of us in community to move into higher frequencies."

I had many things I wanted to know about water dragons, and I quickly asked, "Do you eat anything?"

"Our food comes from the energy sources within the ocean. We no longer consume flesh of any kind. Earlier in our evolution, when some of our dragon brothers left the water and climbed onto the land, our lineage decided to stay in the water and evolve there communally."

I sent him a picture of humpback whales living in pods on Earth and of them being deep dreamers.

"Yes, we know of them," he acknowledged. "Water dragons do not need to travel to other worlds because we can do everything by mind. Now if there are no further questions…"

"Actually, I have one more question," I said. "When I was visiting Kauai, an island on my planet, I met two water dragons. One lived in the ocean and another was blind and lived in a cave. The Hawaiians, humans that is, believe they belong to a lineage just like dragons do. Each Hawaiian lineage has what they call an *amakua*, which is an ancestor who looks after them. The water dragon who lived in the ocean said that he was my amakua, a 'moʻo', on my mother's side."

"Yes, we know of them," replied the huge water dragon, peering at me. "I see your relationship with them and this is why I speak with you. They are an earlier evolution of ours. Like land dragons, we had throwbacks in our evolution, ones that were unable to go forward into higher frequencies. Earlier in our water dragon evolution, we found worlds for them to go to. These are your mo'o. They also are dreamers."

"The blind mo'o lived in a cave in the water and I...?"

"Our caves are not always in the air," he continued, anticipating my question. "Some land-based dragons prefer to have caves anchored on the ground, others want caves high in the mountains, and others like to swim and enter underwater caves. Each lineage chooses caves that reflect their preference."

"Was the mo'o I met blind because of the darkness of the caves?" I inquired.

"No," the water dragon answered. "External sight would have distracted the mo'o from entering the internal state and that is why it was blind. Now our time has come to an end."

With his last words, he called a wave to embrace him and slid into the water, signaling the end of our audience.

Jake waited until the water dragon had fully departed before speaking. "We are greatly honored that the wise one came to speak with us. Water dragons don't wish to devote time to an embodied existence and even our mature land dragons don't often have audiences with them. Water dragons believe that speaking with us land dragons reduces their frequency and delays their goal of leaving bodily existence."

"Are they close to leaving their bodily existence?" I inquired.

"They move into invisibility which only our old, old ones can do. We don't press the water dragons to join our conclaves. However, every millennium or so an old one will come to update us on their progress. When that happens, we must have a conclave by the water and then the water dragon is continually embraced by the water. You have received a great gift and done a lot today and I think it's best to stop."

"I've enjoyed meeting your fledgling friends and now the water dragon. I'm curious about who we'll meet next." I was hinting for a preview of what Jake was planning,

He only smiled and deflected my question. "You'll find out but not today. I'm trying to line up something special, however, it's a bit tricky. Anyway, you're very exhausted. Rest."

Having whetted my appetite for more, Jake disappeared.

Journey to the Lower Dragon World

As the sun rose, I was preparing to go to the dragon world for the 'something special', which Jake had promised, when he popped into my inner vision.

"Don't bother coming," he said. "We're not staying here today. We're expected elsewhere."

"Where elsewhere?" I inquired. I couldn't help but notice he looked nervous.

"You'll enjoy it. It's something you wanted," he replied, trying unsuccessfully to reassure me. Jake was standing on his back legs, holding what looked like a scroll in his right front claw.

"What's that you've got?" I asked, pointing at the scroll.

"It's an introduction," he replied, clearing his throat.

"An introduction to whom?"

"To the dragon we'll be speaking with today who is … well, he's not in my world."

"Could I hazard a guess that he is a lower-frequency dragon that we will be meeting in his dragon world?"

"Yes, that would be correct," replied my dragon brother. "However, don't worry, I'm going with you. I have an introduction and these papers to guarantee our safety."

"Our safety?" I exclaimed. "If I remember correctly, you told me that those dragons don't like humans and, moreover, that they are gigantic. I admit I'm curious, but couldn't you send me holographic images so we could stay here safely?"

"We'll be perfectly safe. Our ambassador to the lower-frequency dragon world has requested that their ambassador meet with us. It's all here in the papers," he continued, waving the scroll at me.

"How do we get there?" I asked.

"That's simple. I'm going to take you."

"Do I need to change into a dragon body?"

"Of course you do. I can't take you looking like a human."

"And should I change into the same dragon body I've been using in your world?"

"That's a stupid question. That IS your dragon body."

"And am I going to have a moment to adjust before we land?"

"That's enough questions. You're overthinking this," Jake said, showing frustration. "I want you to visualize the two of us going together to the lower-frequency dragon world. It's as simple as that. Just like you travel to our world, imagine yourself traveling to their world with me."

I imagined placing myself within his aura to go with him to the lower-frequency dragon world, which I knew was still in a higher frequency than my world. I don't want to make it sound as if I was unwilling because I was quite excited to learn about those dragons first-hand. However, underneath my excitement, I had strong reservations about their acceptance of a human … even if I was in my dragon form.

Jake heard my doubts and volunteered, "I have concerns too. You're not the only one who will be in a foreign land. They are much larger than our race and I'm still a fledgling and fledglings don't move between our worlds. And don't forget, I'm responsible for you. So what do you have to worry about?"

From his words, I realized that he also was nervous about being accepted which heightened my unease. We didn't have time to speak further before we alighted in a lush forest reminiscent of Jurassic Park. Images of dinosaurs resembling Tyrannosaurus Rex flashed through my mind and I expected them to crash through the bushes at any moment. Jake and I stood glued to the landing spot, wondering what we should do next. We didn't wait long before we heard branches breaking and that sound coming closer. My brother stepped towards me, and I was unsure who was protecting whom as a massive emerald dragon emerged from the undergrowth.

This dragon was much larger than the ancient ruby-red dragon I'd met in Iceland, making it at least three times our size. He was broader and heavier with a sizable paunch and he wore a wreath with red berries on his head which, I surmised, signified his official ambassador status. He walked on two jumbo-sized back legs and his front legs were smaller (in relation to his size) than those of the higher-frequency dragons. In his talons, he carried a similar scroll to Jakes'. He peered at us with disappointment and it was a fair assumption that it had to do with the youth of my young friend.

Jake registered the stranger's displeasure and decided to ameliorate the situation by extending his scroll. "You can see, Sir, that we have been permitted by our ambassador, Sigmagupakin, to visit your world. Here's our letter of introduction requesting your assistance."

The mature dragon took the extended scroll and gave Jake his. Both dragons unfurled their respective scrolls in tandem and began to read them. I didn't understand why this protocol was necessary when all they needed to do was speak with each other and tried to hold back a nervous giggle, which I had no doubt would be totally inappropriate.

Picking up on my amusement, the strange dragon locked eyes with me and stated, "Protocols must be adhered to as we are not friendly to humans and have only intermittent contact with the other dragon world."

Although he spoke to me using the same kind of telepathy that I was used to in the higher dragon world, his words carried more force. His chastisement told me in no uncertain terms that I'd better shape up or the purpose for our visit would be in danger of failing.

Neither Jake nor I knew what protocols to use next, therefore, we waited for a sign from the mature dragon.

"By way of formal introductions," he began, sensing our dilemma, "I am Hisssofforwas, the ambassador, and it would be unlikely that anyone other than me would welcome you. As you know by our history," he continued, addressing me, "we and humans have not always gotten along. There is only one reason that I would meet with a human and a fledgling (he looked disparagingly at Jake) and that is to give you a fair account of our world so that you, a human, (he looked disparagingly at me) can put a positive version of us in the book which your ambassador says you are writing."

Hisssofforwas looked from Jake to me, wondering if either of us was capable of speech. I was intimidated and experiencing difficulty retaining my dragon shape and was relieved when Jake rescued the situation.

"Sir, I'm Jaakelousekindvron and we appreciate you taking time from your other duties to speak with such young, inexperienced ones as us."

That was the ticket. Jake found a way to ameliorate the situation by appealing to the mature dragon's sense of pride and expertise.

"Hmmm... Your name tells me you must be Drakekindvron's nestling but, being indigo, you don't look at all like him. When I was young, he was my mentor to the ruby dragons in your world. Is he well? Oh, I forgot that you don't keep in touch with your sires as we do here."

Wow, I was thinking, that was an interesting piece of history about Jake's sire but I didn't have time to dwell on that information. My dragon brother bristled at being referred to as a nestling and I knew he was about to lose the points he had just gained when, luckily, Hisssofforwas said, "Let's get on with the tour. Follow me."

The stocky dragon set off down a path to our right and expected us to fall in behind him. The environment was a complete contrast to that of the higher-frequency dragon world. The moisture and abundant vegetation reminded me of our rainforests on Earth and my brother had a broad smile on his face as he happily clomped along the muddy path.

'Hisss' I thought, giving him a nickname — not that I had the impudence to share it with him — crashed through the undergrowth seemingly unaware of the debris that was tumbling around us in his wake. Not in the mood to complain, we wove around falling branches and soon emerged from the forest into a long valley with cliffs on both sides and, in the middle, a settlement where dragons of all ages, sizes, and genders mingled. What a difference from the solitary and quiet high-frequency world I'd become used to.

Jake stared with his mouth agape and I signaled to him to close it as Hisss led us through the menagerie. Noticing our approach, the assorted dragons became silent and stared at us. You could tell by their attention that they'd never seen such a young higher-frequency dragon before. Jake, holding himself erect, attempted to become as large as possible, while I concentrated on maintaining my dragon body.

"Look, it's a human," one of the younger dragons exclaimed, pointing at me. I thought I'd done a good job of maintaining my dragon body, but either my scent or aura or something else, had given me away.

"Amazing," another young one commented, moving closer with the intention of touching me. Approximately Jake's age, but double in size, I didn't feel safe given the dicey history of humans with low-frequency dragons.

"These are our GUESTS," Hisss interrupted, halting in his tracks. "Get on with your business."

The young dragon apologized and backed away in deference, indicating that the dragon ambassador was well respected. Hisss resumed walking through the huge, staring dragons and headed towards a structure on the far side of the settlement.

Looking around, I noticed that the valley was honeycombed with caves from the ground to far up on the cliffs. Unlike the other dragon world, wooden structures extended from the entrances of each cave and each structure was unique. Some were square, others rectangular or circular, and various trees and bushes were woven into each structure. This village with its lush, earthy structures was more appealing to me than the arid landscape of the other dragon world. Jake, it seemed, agreed because he exuded waves of pleasure as he surveyed the surroundings.

Hisss halted in front of a cave located on the ground. There, a youngish female dragon and two little ones waited.

"This is Murmastosis, my current mate and my current nestlings," Hisss said by way of introduction.

I would have liked to ask what current meant, but I didn't want to be rude.

"Make yourselves comfortable," Murmastosis said, waving us towards a sand pit steaming with warm coals.

Doing as directed, we settled into the pit and she placed rubies and garnets, which I assumed were for energy, in front of us.

"Thank you for your warm welcome," said Jake courteously to Murmastosis. I admired his tactfulness, given what for him was an unknown situation.

"Not unknown," he whispered telepathically. "Our teacher has holographically shown us these structures and told us about the appropriate behaviors in this world."

At that moment, Hisss entered the sand pit with us and his nestlings cuddled into his pudgy side.

Jake's eyes widened with surprise at the affection the nestlings displayed.

Hisss noticed and commented to Jake, "Unlike your world, in our world sires maintain close contact with their offspring. We find this settles and nurtures them in ways that you would find distasteful."

Hisss took on the role of the knowledgeable elder telling the youngster how to improve and Jake, I was happy to see, accepted his teaching with good grace. Until now, I'd silently observed this world and the interactions as I'd not wanted to get off on the wrong foot. I now felt more comfortable and decided to ask a question.

"In what ways do you teach your offspring, Sir?" I asked.

"As you probably know," he replied, turning his attention towards me, "our world is in a lower astral frequency which is closer to the frequency of Earth than that of the higher dragon world."

I nodded in understanding and he continued in a fatherly tone, "We respect love, patience, loyalty, compassion, and other noble qualities, and strive to develop these. We've discovered that, if we are physically affectionate with our nestlings and fledglings, they develop these qualities more easily."

"We've learned the same thing in the human world," I responded, trying to create a bridge between us.

Meanwhile, off to the side, I noticed some fledgling males carrying a branch and urging Jake to join them in what looked to be a game involving physical contact. Although he loved to try new things and wanted to join them, he was aware of his physical disadvantage, being half the size of the other fledglings, and hesitated.

Hisss recognized Jake's dilemma. Calling the fledglings over to the pit, he proposed, "Instead of physically tackling each other to get the branch, I suggest you only touch each other with the branch and whoever gets touched is out of the game. The winner is the one who remains untouched with the branch. That way, our GUEST can join you."

The fledglings looked at each other dubiously given that physical tackling appeared to be high on their list of priorities. However, taking a good look at skinny, smaller Jake, and at the urging of the word GUEST, they agreed. By unspoken consent, the largest fledgling took the branch.

Jake was up like a shot and into the center of their group staying well clear of the branch. The large ruby fledgling holding the branch raced after Jake but, when he couldn't catch him, he tagged an emerald one who was in his way. The emerald one was out and the large ruby one went after Jake again. Jake quickly darted between the sapphire and indigo males and the ruby dragon, seeing an opportunity, tagged the sapphire one. Two fledglings remained and the ruby youngster gained speed as he tore after Jake. It was not looking good for my small dragon brother when the sapphire fledgling set off after both of them and, intercepting his ruby friend, grabbed the branch from his talon. Seeing the ruby's predicament, the others fell about laughing, clearly the game's rules were changing as they played.

The large ruby youngster took off with the sapphire after him. Jake stood where he was, puzzling what to do, when the sapphire veered off and tagged him and gave him the branch. Laughing at being tricked, Jake set off after the large ruby fledgling who ran too fast for Jake to catch. Jake finally stopped and, gasping, accepted defeat. The others ran up to him and clapped him on the back. He buckled under their enthusiasm, but remained standing, proud that he'd held his own. Returning to the pit, he collapsed exhausted.

"That's the way to make friends," said Hisss in approval, staring at me to see what I intended to do as an encore.

"Nothing," I said out loud. "With any strenuous activity I'll revert to my human form and be pulverized. And then what will the entry in my book say about you? I can tell you right now it won't be favorable."

"Good point," Hisss replied agreeably.

"Do you have another suggestion about what you'd like to do?" he persisted, raising his right eyebrow.

Racking my brain and looking at the young female who was watching me, I said, "I'd like to speak with Murmastosis."

"Of course," Hisss agreed good-naturedly. Grabbing the two nestlings, one in each talon, he climbed out of the warm pit. Hisss nodded to Jake to ask if he wanted to accompany him. My dragon brother looked at me with a 'Can I stay' look and I agreed. After all, this was his chance to learn more about their world and I wouldn't deprive him of the opportunity.

Murmastosis looked at me and then at Jake and waited for one of us to ask her something. Strange as it may seem, I didn't know what to ask her because I didn't want to do or say anything improper.

Jake came to the rescue. "If you don't mind me inquiring, could you tell us about the relationship between females and males in your world?"

Such an obvious question for a young male dragon to ask and the young female smiled thinking the same thought as me.

"In our world, females are equal partners choosing a mate and raising the nestlings," she replied with pride and authority.

Being emerald and much younger than Hisss, I was also curious to learn more about gender roles in the lower-frequency dragon world.

"Hisss said you were his current mate. What did he mean?" I asked as tactfully as possible.

"I'm his fifth mate and it's his fourth bunch of nestlings," Murmastosis responded. "But he's my first mate. Younger females and males often have older mates to properly teach them how to be good mates and how to raise offspring."

She smiled coyly at Jake as she spoke and I sensed a change in the direction the conversation was going.

"Hmmm...Hmmm...," Jake began, getting to his real question. "Would females here find males from my world desirable as mates?"

"It depends on what he offers in the way of desirable qualities," she responded, inviting further discussion.

"Hmmm…Hmmm…," Jake persisted. "Is it desirable for an emerald female, for example, to ever think of an indigo mate as attractive?"

"Certainly," she replied coquettishly and I could see where this was going. "However, if she had nestlings to raise, she'd want them fledged first. I'm sure you understand."

"Oh yes," replied Jake oozing understanding. "And it would have to be the right time when both dragons were adults, don't you think?"

Oh my gawd, how had I become an eavesdropper on courting?

"Yes, that's correct," the lovely emerald female replied, demurely dropping her head. "And in our world, both males and females may have many mates in a lifetime. Is it the same in yours?"

"Absolutely," Jake responded, dragging himself to his full height.

"Great," I said turning first to her and then to him. "I've learned so much. Thanks so much for sharing."

"And now Jaakelousekindvron, it's time to return to your world, don't you think?" I gave him a telepathic nudge and he got the point.

"Please give our best wishes to the ambassador and thank him for receiving us," he said courteously to Murmastosis, before adding with a twinkle in his eye. "I look forward to seeing you again."

I nodded goodbye and, grabbing him mentally, thrust him back into his world while I returned to mine.

Perhaps I've headed off some breach of dragon etiquette, I thought to myself, as I reviewed what had transpired between Jake and the young female. Overall, I thought we'd done well, but I looked forward to hearing what my dear dragon brother had to say for himself about his courting when next we'd meet.

My Brood Mother

Worried about the repercussions of Jake's behavior, I didn't sleep well. When I opened my eyes on a new day, I quickly transformed my human form into my familiar dragon body and went to his cave. He crouched there awaiting me with a stern expression.

"I didn't take kindly to you mentally pushing me," he huffed, getting to his feet. "That for dragons is very offensive and lacking in respect."

"What were you doing flirting with another dragon's mate and, to boot, in a foreign world? Oops, did I neglect to mention that it was the ambassador's mate?" I countered, lecturing him.

"When you think like a human, you don't understand," he said.

"And don't scold, it's very unbecoming," he added, not taking my concern seriously.

"Then explain. What don't I understand?" I asked confused.

"I offered Murmastosis a compliment. And as you could see by her response I, being a higher-frequency dragon, would be welcome as a future mate … when I become an adult of course."

"Which is?" I inquired.

"I'll be mature in a few hundred years at which time she will still be young and lovely and smaller than most other females in the lower-frequency world. In other words, desirable."

"That's a good point," I admitted. "Murmastosis did say that she is Hisss's fifth mate, so I understand that having many mates is fine in both of your dragon worlds. But, what I don't understand is why you are making such a serious commitment at such a young age with a dragon who's not even from your race?"

"Again...you don't understand," he replied, with exaggerated patience. "I think it's time for you to meet our brood mother. She can better explain everything to you. I, on the other hand, will be with my fledgling friends who will be congratulating me."

Jake sent out an urgent call to our brood mother and, shaking his head at me, walked to the entrance of the cave and took flight.

He was right. I didn't have a clue how to interpret his behavior. I'd waited a long time to speak with my brood mother as the last time was only a remembered vision of her downloading her ancestral memories into me and nothing that I'd call a conversation. Nevertheless, I regretted the circumstances and wondered if I'd made a grievous error in judgment. I was busy rehashing the unpleasant conversation with my dragon brother when a mature indigo female landed at the cave entrance. Peering into the darkness, she saw me and, kicking up dust with her large talons, walked forward. I was glued to the spot. She was larger than Jake and I was in her cave. Having no idea what to say or do, I did nothing.

"Come now," she said, gazing at me with amber eyes. "There's no need to be nervous. Don't I know you as well as that nest brother of yours."

"I have memories of being in your cave when Jake was hatching, however meeting you in the present is different," I responded.

"It's only different to your human senses. For dragons, as you should know by now, time is fluid and we can experience past, present, or future, by mentally flowing through the current of time. But that's not why I'm here. I understand from Jaakelousekindvron that you need instruction on male and female relationships."

My dragon mother smiled indulgently, putting me at ease. She was beautiful by dragon standards. Her indigo scales glowed with health and she had a warm, welcoming disposition. I could think of many questions I wanted to ask but chose to go directly to the central question that kept nagging at me.

"How did you brood me? After all, I'm a human, not a dragon, so I don't understand if I was in an egg or what?"

"Hahaha," she responded good-naturedly. "Humans have such strange questions. In the higher astral world, you can take any form you wish. The beings who oversee our dragon evolution coordinate with the beings who oversee human and other evolutions. They knew that you were searching in your astral and causal bodies for a conscious experience of our world because you, like Jaakelousekindvron, were destined to be bridges between evolutions. Your sire and I were created through generations to host both of you together in the nest."

"Oh my," I responded in awe. "Through generations?"

"Of course, all is known by great beings for generations. It's not only your evolution, it's all evolutions. Have you never considered this?"

"I suppose I haven't," I answered, "but I am now. Back to my question, was I in an egg?"

"Yes, in our high astral world, you were in an egg."

"In a waking dream, I remember being in your cave and under your breast, but I was a human and not a dragon. How do you explain that?"

"You awoke in your human form in our astral world and didn't understand how to interpret your experience. However, it was not the right time for you to consciously meet us."

"You're right," I replied. "Earlier in my life I wouldn't have understood how I could put on a dragon body and travel to your world. If I hadn't explored the elemental world and met people on Earth who were hybrids of various evolutions, such as elves, angels, and dragons, I never would have believed I could be in a dragon egg in the higher astral world."

My brood mother's words had rung with layers of truth and this truth had settled into every cell of my body. She watched me with approval and I readied my second question.

"Do you have other nestlings and, if so, are they of other races too?"

"I currently don't have other nestlings, but I have had twice in the past. They were those of our dragon race. I needed to gain experience with nestlings before I was given the responsibility for brooding you and your nest brother together as both of you have a mission to create a bridge between the human and dragon worlds. As you've seen, brooding involves more than keeping eggs warm. Brood mothers must give the nestlings the memories of their ancestors and this takes practice to learn the appropriate timing in teaching nestlings."

I was curious to know. "Was my astral sire the same as the sires for your other nestlings?"

"Not at all," she replied. "The first sire was indigo like me and quite old; the second was sapphire and much younger. I needed experience of other lineages and temperaments before mating with your ancient ruby sire."

"Ah, I have a difficult question." I hesitated as I didn't want to offend her. "I don't want you to think I'm ungrateful to be learning from Jake, but why didn't I receive an older, more experienced dragon, like you."

"Jaakelousekindvron has an ancient soul and he is destined to be a progressive leader among us. I'm honored to have been his brood mother. He is more flexible than older dragons and more compassionate than most of us. He has all the qualities and information you need for your task and what he doesn't know, he has enough inventiveness that he can find out."

"This brings me to the next question," I inquired "Jake seems to be interested in mating with a youngish, smallish, emerald, lower-frequency female who also happens to be the current mate of the ambassador to your world. Jake made his future intentions clear to her and she was definitely interested. Is this kind of behavior acceptable?"

"He's clever to have already put this plan in place. In doing so, he makes it clear that one of his goals will be to work closely with the lower-frequency dragons. And to choose the current mate of their ambassador is brilliant. Surely, you can see this?" my brood mother asked questioning, not Jake's, but my judgment.

"He wanted me to speak with you because I doubted him," I confessed. "Now, thanks to your explanation, I more fully understand the differences between human and dragon ways of mating and having relationships."

She stared at me and I could tell she was weighing something in her mind. "I have a suggestion," she said finally. "I think it would be good for you to meet the ancient, wise ruby dragon who sired you."

"If possible," I said, overwhelmed with this prospect, "I'd prefer to meet him another day. Today I'm feeling insecure about my ability to understand dragons as I've made quite a blunder with Jake."

"That's to be expected," my brood mother replied. "You're not a full dragon in the current way you have been visiting our world. You and Jaakelousekindvron are both in training."

"Training?" I queried, mentally requesting her to say more.

"Jaakelousekindvron will become a bridge between many evolutions. He's starting with humans and you were nestlings together to give him a head start in understanding your race."

Her answer led me to wonder how many years dragons live so that Jake had time to fulfill his purpose.

"Many thousands of years," she replied, answering my unvoiced question.

"That's nice for him, but humans have short lives, so it might have been better for both of you to have chosen a longer living race."

"You are short-sighted," she interjected. "To be fully grounded, Jaakelousekindvron must start his training in a dense physical world, hence, Earth. Secondly, he must become effective in working in the lower astral world, hence, the lower-frequency dragon world. All beings, including you, evolve physically, astrally, causally, and even beyond this. He and you have been working together on all of these frequencies. Even when your puny physical human life ends, you will continue to evolve astrally and causally as you are doing even as we speak."

"I know that," I replied, miffed at being lectured to.

"We've offered you a wonderful opportunity to become conscious in the lower and higher astral frequencies," my brood mother replied indulgently. "There are human masters interacting with our highly evolved dragons in the causal world and you are in training to join them."

"Are you sure?" I asked.

"It's your destiny as a bridge between evolutions. That's why you were working first with the elementals in a lower-frequency astral world and now with us. You and Jaakelousekindvron are both in training to do this and this training spans thousands of years."

I attempted to absorb all she'd said. I knew in theory that all beings evolve through ever higher frequencies. Furthermore, in examining my life's work with humans, elementals, and now dragons, it made sense that my soul's purpose was to continue this. Still, living day to day, I seldom thought about my soul's destiny.

My brood mother did not rush me. Instead, she quietly followed my inner thoughts.

"I've said as much as I wish to say," she said with finality. "Your sire is further ahead in evolution than me so it's best you meet with him to learn about how dragons evolve to higher consciousness."

"Will you or Jake go with me?" I queried hopefully as I didn't want to go by myself.

My brood mother answered abruptly, "It's inappropriate. Neither I nor Jaakelousekindvron would disturb him."

"And I should? That doesn't make sense, " I countered, increasingly unwilling to act on her suggestion.

She was amused and replied, "Once again, you don't understand dragon protocol. Let me explain. First, as a human, you are a guest in our world. Second, he is your sire and you've never met him and you should. Third, he is a wayshower to higher worlds and, as such, you need to speak with him. Fourth,..."

"Alright," I interjected, getting the message. "There's no need for fourth or fifth, I agree. However, I prefer to meet him another day as I'm quite exhausted. But before you leave, I'd greatly appreciate your instruction about how and where to meet my sire?"

"Your intuition IS correct," my brood mother said as she noticed my fatigue. "It would be better for you to meet him another day. So, let's proceed with instruction, shall we?"

I nodded in agreement and she continued, "Meditate deeply in a quiet place to reach even higher frequencies than you've done already. Then, reach out mentally and ask for permission to visit him."

"Sorry to interrupt, but, seeing I've never met him, how will I contact him? I don't want to disturb another dragon."

My brood mother explained. "You're his kin. He will recognize your call and you will recognize his energy signature. Don't complicate it. Overthinking is such a useless human trait."

With her last words, she rose to her feet to leave.

"Thanks for describing the process," I replied gratefully. "Could I ask one further question?"

"Which is?"

Now that I had her full attention, I asked, "Please excuse any insult, but what exactly are your qualities that you were chosen to be my brood mother?"

Opening her wings fully to expose their underside, she revealed how blue they were. "Through the sapphire lineage, I was bred to be compassionate, which combined with the spiritual indigo lineage made me perfect to raise both you and Jake, as you call him."

"I appreciate your compassion and generosity and am grateful that you were chosen as my brood mother. Will we meet again?"

"Perhaps," she answered, getting to her feet. "Our paths are not identical. Despite your dominant indigo coloring, your and Jaakelousekindvron's paths are, in many ways, more aligned to that of your sire."

"And what is your path?" I asked, attempting to have one more question answered.

"Enough," she interjected. "I'm needed elsewhere. Important questions will be answered by your sire."

Smiling at me one last time, she walked briskly to the cave's entrance and flew off.

Quite sure Jake could answer some of my remaining questions, I waited to see if he'd return. It did not happen. I assumed he'd decided not to intervene in our brood mother's request that I speak with our sire. Therefore, tired from maintaining a dragon body, I reverted to my human form and returned home.

The Cosmic Dragon

Several days later, on the winter solstice, I was sitting peacefully in the meditation garden with the sun streaming down on me. Although it was late December in Canada, it was as warm as an autumn day. Winter solstice is the first day of the new year when the sun begins to strengthen its way toward the spring. The timing was perfect to meet my dragon sire.

Entering deeper meditation, I was wondering how to contact him when I heard, "I am ready to receive you now."

I could hear him, but not see him. This was a departure from my conversations with all the other dragons I'd met. Still, I had an intuition that there was no time to waste pondering why I couldn't see him. I intuitively knew that cosmic questions, rather than personal questions, would be the most appreciated by him.

"Do you have the equivalent of a winter solstice in the dragon world?" I began fumbling for how to begin.

He replied in a deep wise voice, "Planets and solar systems exist and move within the design of the Source of All. Together, we are joined in the grid of continuous evolution moving from the lowest to the highest frequencies and beyond into the silence of the Source of All. This you can only know in the silence of deep space in what you refer to as the Void, which is the formless existence outside space and time. You first encounter this as an emptiness that is alive with potential. And that's what I choose to discuss with you today."

He paused to make certain I was following him before continuing.

"Seldom do I descend to a low enough frequency to communicate with you or with beings like you. I hesitate as it slows down my evolution which is surrendering all attachments to form worlds. Still, as you are my kin, I could not refuse the call."

"But, Sir, I hadn't called you yet," I responded.

"I know," my sire answered, "but your brood mother placed a call within higher frequencies encapsulating the seed of what you wish to know. Where I exist, all is potential. I no longer feel inclined to manifest because I have only one desire: to unite with the Source of All in greater and greater merging to know and fulfill its bidding away from form. This is the journey I am on. You and your nest brother are the last of my progeny. I was reluctant to leave the formless and return to the form world to fulfill my contracted destiny to fertilize both of you."

"Please, could you tell me how you did this?" I asked politely as I now realized how my questions took him away from the formless realms.

"Mentally," he replied. "When you or any being reaches the level where I exist, all fertilizing happens mentally. There is no longer a need for physical interaction or coitus. There is no desire, only a lingering duty to perform the last role one was designed for in the form world. Thus, I speak with you today to fulfill my contract with the Source of All."

I was concerned that Jake was not benefiting, like I was, from speaking with our sire and I asked, "Sir, why speak only to me? Why not to my nest brother?"

"He understands dragon destiny and the sequence of steps," our sire answered. "Every sacrifice and every progress is taught in the nest, imbued within the memories of your brood mother. He understands, whereas you, being human, do not, therefore necessitating words."

"Are all dragon lineages given this opportunity to move beyond form?" I asked, wanting to fully understand.

"Of course, all dragon lineages and all races in all solar systems and the cosmos are given this opportunity."

"Is it more difficult for a ruby than, let's say, a sapphire or indigo dragon?" I probed, knowing he was a ruby dragon even though I couldn't see him.

"No," he replied. "The ruby has more will and life force energy than dragons in many other lineages. My will is aligned with cosmic will in the higher causal frequencies. That does not mean that other lineages do not have equally desirable qualities that allow them to rise to higher formless existence. Every being must use their strengths and take the opportunities given by the Source of All and follow the path to their conclusion. This is what I am doing."

"Sir, when you were younger, did you ever doubt or hesitate or fall back?" I asked as I've doubted myself and been lazy many times.

"Yes, of course," he replied. "This is a normal stage in the evolutionary process as one refines one's spiritual nature more and more and lets go of the form world. This process increases in speed and becomes more difficult as one gets closer to the formless world. Never doubt that. Thus, it is often difficult for a being to ascertain progress as the being severs each strand to the world of form."

I was fascinated by everything he said and would have liked to speak with him for days, however, I knew this was not to be. Choosing the question uppermost in my mind, I inquired, "What is your function?"

"Function is a word used in lower frequencies," my sire began. "It is a more 'doing' word and I am more 'being'. Nevertheless, I understand your question. I deeply surrender and merge with the Source of All. I am letting go of my identity as a ruby dragon and even as a dragon. Yet, paradoxically, as I am dissolving on one level, I am evolving on another. I am becoming a Star Dragon, a being of the stars.

"In my youth, thousands of years ago in your time," he continued, "I traveled star paths to countless physical and astral worlds. I was curious, perhaps more than most of my kind, to see for myself other environments, other solar systems, and how other evolutions lived. In later years, I became a cosmic traveler far, far, far out on the grid of light to bring knowledge back to the dragon world. Others regarded me as a leader and I became the head of the ruby lineage. On one level, it was an honor and something to be sought. On another, I was fettered by pride and responsibility to my race to stay in the form world. I was fettered when my soul, my deeper self, wished freedom to explore the higher causal realm. Now, once again, I am leaving there to travel the stars, but this time as a Star Dragon."

This was the first time I'd heard this term and I wanted to make certain I understood what he was saying, so I asked, "What is a Star Dragon?"

"You call us the Cosmic Dragon. You have human masters who have moved beyond space and time and so have we dragons."

"But I have seen the Star Dragon, the Cosmic Dragon," I said. "And I still live in the physical world within space and time. How is it possible if the Star Dragon is beyond form?"

"Perceptive nestling," he replied. "I know what you have seen, but *you* do not fully know what you've seen. We, Star Dragons, are not one; we are many who have left form. Yet, some are asked by the Source of All to return to the higher form realms to help with the evolution of planets, solar systems, and the cosmos. This is the role of our brotherhood and sisterhood. Previously, you mentioned the word 'function' and you could say this is our function, although I stress this is not a word that pertains to us. Our role is beyond the thought world. It is a being world. We are united in harmony with the Source of All. I am only in the first stages of this uniting, so I cannot speak from a depth of experience, but I can point the way to this realm. Here, human masters, dragon masters, merpeople, phoenixes, and many others live in a state of potential. They know and breathe in and out the destinies of planets and races."

"It's difficult for me to follow what you're saying." I admitted.

"Of course it is," he said. "Words cannot convey what we are, although we attempt to do so, so that you can glimpse your potential, your soul destiny, not as an individual, but the destiny of your race."

I was still attempting to understand why I had seen the Star Dragons, so I asked, "Do Star Dragons work mostly with dragons?"

"Some do and some do not."

"As you might know, Mahavatar Babaji requested that I write this book about the dragon world. Is he a dragon?"

My sire replied, "He is a dragon. He is also a human. He is a Star Dragon."

"I don't understand how he can be both." I said, seeking clarity.

"I know you don't understand, nestling. Write exactly what I've said and it will become clear to you and others in time. We are finished with our meeting. Be well and fulfill your destiny."

With those last words, he broke the link and moved beyond my hearing. I felt honored that my sire, a Star Dragon, had come to a lower frequency to speak with me and our conversation felt complete.

Last Words

Throughout my experience with my nest brother, brood mother, and sire, I couldn't figure out how I, a human, could be brooded as a dragon. I didn't dispute the accuracy of what each of them had told me or my actual experiences in the dragon world. My unresolved question entirely lay in my attachment to my physical body as a human, which I couldn't reconcile with being physically related to dragons. Only when I'd finished writing the book and had laid this issue to rest did the answer to my question come of its own accord.

I AM A DRAGON in the dragon world!

Up until the moment of my realization, I thought of myself as a human inside a dragon body when I visited the dragon world. What had changed was that I now recognized that I had another existence as a dragon living in the dragon world. Previously, I could not allow myself to accept this realization because, in doing so, it negated my identification as a human. Now, however, I knew that I was a human in the third-dimensional reality of my Earth life and I was a dragon in the higher astral frequency of the dragon world. My dragon brother had alluded to this when we were first getting to know each other, but it had not taken root in me. I wasn't ready to know.

This revelation opened the door for me to more deeply comprehend what Jesus meant when he said, "In my Father's house are many mansions." [4] His Father's house is the cosmos and each mansion is another world. And…, if I am a dragon in the dragon world, I could simultaneously be a merperson in the merworld and another being in another world. These existences could all exist concurrently in different worlds and frequencies.

One question remained. Why had my dragon brother and the others pretended that I was a human when I visited their world in my dragon body? Even as I asked myself this question, I knew the answer. They saw me as I saw myself, which was as a human inside a dragon body. Furthermore, I realized my dragon family was aware that I was a full dragon in their world and waited for me to experience this revelation for myself. All beings, humans, dragons, or otherwise, must discover by themselves what I had now ascertained. No one can help anyone else to move from theory to deep inner knowing. I had entered a new place, a paradigm shift in consciousness, a gigantic 'aha' that happens if we are very lucky and have a moment of grace and clarity.

My next knowing was that Mahavatar Babaji, by requesting that I write about the dragon world, had offered me the key to open the door to this new paradigm. He not only wanted me to gain knowledge, he energetically catapulted me into this new reality! And I, like all beings, had free will to say 'yay' or 'nay'. Thank heavens, Babaji was patient with the time I took to fulfill his request as I balanced my human desires with soul priorities as a multidimensional being.

All of these revelations occurred at the same time. Gossamer thin films that separated me from each knowing instantaneously dissolved without effort.

You may be wondering, based on the hints in my story, how I could not see that I had another life as a dragon in the dragon world. I was a victim of what is referred to in psychology as 'confirmation bias', which is the tendency to search for, interpret, favor, and recall information in a way that confirms or supports one's prior beliefs or values. We cannot see outside the box...outside of our own beliefs. Even scientists are known to deny the results of their experiments if they do not agree with their preconceptions. In doing so, they also have confirmation bias.

This is what happened to me because the answer, staring me in the face, was so shocking that I must have subconsciously known, that if I believed I was a dragon, many of my previous beliefs, those that gave me a stable foundation for my human life, would be overturned. When you are in any given paradigm, everything conforms to the beliefs of that paradigm, providing a sense of security and comfort that you know how to function. When an idea or experience enters from a new paradigm, the idea can be confusing and threatening to your existing paradigm. So, the tendency is to resist, even negate the incoming information.

My old paradigm had eroded piece by piece throughout my conversations with the dragons. I had clung to my human identity because to believe that I was simultaneously a dragon was too threatening. Changing this one belief had a cascading effect of dissolving my old paradigm where I had one identity. In the new paradigm, I had several identities and lives in many different worlds. This may sound like an exciting adventure on the surface, and it is, but if you look deeper, you will realize that it consists of an unparalleled journey into the unknown — not something with which humans feel comfortable because it means learning a new set of rules and actions.

I hadn't spoken with Jake, my dragon brother, for several days and there had been no goodbyes when he'd left me with our brood mother. I now recognized that he had abided with Spirit's timing and had to wait for this revelation to awaken in me before he could or would speak with me again. Previously, I was a visitor to his world. I now knew I was a resident.

End Notes

Chapter 3 - How Dragons Travel in Space and Time

[1] Tanis Helliwell's book *Good Morning Henry: An In-Depth Journey with the Body Intelligence* assists individuals to work with their body spirit.

[2] Paramahansa Yogananda, *The Autobiography of a Yogi*, Self-Realization Fellowship, Los Angeles, 1946, printing 2011, p. 354-355.

Chapter 9 - Dragons and Holograms

[3] Tanis Helliwell's book *Decoding Your Destiny: Keys to Humanity's Spiritual Transformation* is a helpful resource in learning about the stages that humanity has evolved through and our next stage in evolution.

Chapter 20 - Last Words

[4] John 14:2-6 KJV

Acknowledgments

I am grateful to Prajnaparamita and Christoph Wasser, who trusted me to tell the story of how the dragon intersected their lives. Without their support, this book would be very different.

Thanks to Jenny Lou Linley who reviewed the unedited manuscript and provided many suggestions to improve the book and to Tracey Schavone who welcomed me to her home where I did, yet, another edit.

Donna Miniely lent her eagle eye to the still-evolving manuscript and her suggestions and those of Margaret Mills were excellent. Thanks also to Marc Vallee who requested clarification of the various astral realms in which dragons, elementals, and humans live and to Janet Rouss who suggested cover ideas and encouraged flying lessons.

Nita Kay Alvarez, a dragon hybrid friend for over three decades, did the final edit and adapted the dragon image of Jake. And, as always, my thanks to Melany Hallam who masterfully completed the layout and finished cover of the book.

wee ar ~~perteaof~~ hem partners.
repairy ar relatursip to hem

Crystal Keeps   They r
                  abby
                  reppers

Galactic   4 Gaic
& Element Drugs.

L his   cut off

+

Soph Serpti
hejent frepers

t lweer frepers

v drygon

My ehrt a eeg frepers.

About the Author

TANIS HELLIWELL has seen higher realms and spoken with Masters, angels and elementals since childhood. Walking in many worlds, she led tours to sacred sites for two decades, was a management consultant working with universities, government, and business for over 30 years, and conducted a psychotherapy practice specializing in spiritual transformation.

She founded the International Institute for Transformation (IIT) in 2000, offering programs to assist individuals in becoming conscious creators to work with the spiritual laws that govern our world. Her gift is assisting others to develop a soul-infused personal life in harmony with the Earth.

Her knowledge and understanding of other worlds and spiritual realms can be found in some of her most popular books: *Summer with the Leprechauns, The Leprechaun's Story, Hybrids: So You Think You Are Human, The High Beings of Hawaii,* and *Good Morning Henry.*

To write to the author, order books or mp3s, or for information on upcoming workshops, please contact:

TANIS HELLIWELL

1766 Hollingsworth Rd.,

Powell River, BC., Canada V8A 0M4

tanis@tanishelliwell.com

tanishelliwell.com | myspiritualtransformation.com

facebook.com/Tanis.Helliwell

Printed in Great Britain
by Amazon

41399849R00119